I0091319

Malthouse Monographs on Africa

Editor: Dafe Otobo, DPhil (Oxford),
Professor, University of Lagos, Lagos, Nigeria

Advisory Editorial Board

Professor Adele Jinadu, Centre for Advanced Social Science, Port Harcourt, Nigeria.
Professor John Ohiorhenuan, UNDP, New York
Professor Eddie Webster, University of Witwatersrand, Johannesburg, South Africa
Gavin Williams, St Peter's College, University of Oxford, UK

Malthouse Monographs on Africa

Malthouse Monographs on Africa are peer-reviewed works on Africa covering the six main areas of a) social sciences and development studies; b) history, law and international relations; c) environmental and agricultural studies; d) gender, refugee and conflict studies; e) strategic and defence studies; and f) labour and trades unions.

The Monographs are intended to provide an arena for free contestation of ideas and as outlet for research and empirical studies on Africa in the areas indicated above. The monographs thus have no links with, nor funded by, any African government or political party. Nor do the views expressed in them represent those of the editorial board.

Works for consideration may be of purely theoretical, or historical or applied in nature or policy-oriented. Such may be sent directly to the Series Editor as electronic files (dafeotobo2002@yahoo.co.uk) in Microsoft Word Rich Text format, or to the publishers (malthouse_press@yahoo.com). Diskettes and hardcopies may also be sent to the publishers at the address on the imprint page. The aim is to publish accepted works within three months.

Malthouse Monographs on Africa
Numbers 1 – 9

Guest Series Editor: Dayo Oluyemi-Kusa,
Director, External Conflict Prevention & Resolution,
Institute for Peace and Conflict Resolution, The
Presidency, Abuja, Nigeria

- Rotimi T. Suberu, *Institutional structure and process of government in Nigeria, 1985-1993*
- R. A. Akindele, *Federalism under General Babangida's administration in Nigeria*
- Dele Olowu & Kunle Awotokun, *Local government and the IBB administration*
- Cyril Obi, *The Nigerian private sector under adjustment and crisis 1985-1993*
- Bola A. Akinterinwa, *General Ibrahim Babangida's legacy: the domestic and international dimensions*
- Nereus I. Nwosu, *Nigeria's foreign policy under General Babangida*
- Antonia T. Oko-Osi, *Corruption and corrupt practices: institutionalization and legitimation under the Babangida Administration*
- Oyeleye Oyediran & Babafemi Badejo, *The military and democracy in Nigeria: the Political Bureau Report*
- Adekunle Amuwo, *Politics of the annulment of June 12 presidential election in Nigeria*

Malthouse Press Limited
43 Onitana Street, Off Stadium Hotel Road,
Surulere, Lagos, Lagos State
E-mail: malthouse_press@yahoo.com
malthouse_lagos@yahoo.co.uk
Tel: +234 (01) -773 53 44; 0802 364 2402

All rights reserved. No part of this publication may be reproduced,
transmitted, transcribed, stored in a retrieval system or translated into any
language or computer language, in any form or by any means, electronic,
mechanical, magnetic, chemical, thermal, manual or otherwise, without the
prior consent in writing of Malthouse Press Limited, Lagos, Nigeria.

This book is sold subject to the condition that it shall not by way of trade,
or otherwise, be lent, re-sold, hired out, or otherwise circulated without the
publisher's prior consent in writing, in any form of binding or cover other than
in which it is published and without a similar condition, including this
condition, being imposed on the subsequent purchaser.

© Malthouse Monographs on Africa 2007
First Published 2007
ISBN 978 023 236 2

Distributors:
African Books Collective Ltd
Email: abc@africanbookscollective.com
Website: http://www.africanbookscollective.com

Guest Editor's comment

All the Monographs in this series attempt to explore and document events, policies and impact of the General Ibrahim Babangida-led military regime in Nigeria, covering the period 1985 to 1993. These contributions were originally for a book edited by me on that regime but other considerations, especially that of comprehensiveness of coverage of arguably the most momentous phase in Nigeria's post-Civil War socio-political development, led to the shelving of that idea. It was thought that a more useful scope or coverage might be achieved through a continuing development of Monographs on different facets of Nigerian society under this regime – a feat which may only be possible in a book so voluminous and whose cost might be such as to be out of the reach of the intended audience.

I should like to thank all the contributors who have waited this long to see their work in print, a fate that is unlikely to befall the contributors of the other titles currently in preparation. I am grateful to the publishers for including these titles in Malthouse Monographs for Africa family.

Dayo Oluyemi-Kusa

Corruption and corrupt practices: *institutionalization and legitimation under the Babangida Administration*

Antonia T. Oko-osi, PhD

*Nigerian Institute for Economic and Social Research
Ibadan, Nigeria.*

No. 7

Contents

Introduction

It is widely acknowledged that corruption is the bane of Nigerian politics and society. Under the Babangida regime especially, corruption and mismanagement reached unprecedented proportions.[1] This chapter is an attempt to examine the phenomenon of corruption in the public sector of Nigeria with particular reference to the period between 1985 and 1993. We lay emphasis on the public sector because it is a truism that government which is supposed to fight and defeat corruption is the kernel of the problem in Nigeria. The Centre for Advanced Social Sciences (CASS) put it succinctly when it said,

> ...It is government that has contributed most to lowering the moral tone of society in Nigeria. It is in government that corruption thrives most, wasting resources we need, defeating all prospects of democracy and developments all sense of patriotism and turning all of us into hardened cynics with no concern for the public good, no faith in public morality or even its possibility.[2]

It is appropriate therefore that a thorough look at the corruption problem between 1985 and 1993 begin with an incisive examination of the government itself. To achieve this objective, section two contains theoretical perspectives in which some postulations, causes and forms of corruption with particular reference to Nigeria are briefly enunciated.

---

[1] *African Guardian* November 1, 1993, p. 2.
[2] Centre for Advanced Social Sciences (CASS). Brief to Participants for the Seminar on Corruptions. Port-Harcourt, December 2-4, 1993.

Section three does an overview of the corruption situation in the country under Military President General Ibrahim Badamasi Babangida's administration. To do this, few case studies of corruption are presented and analysed. A critique of government provisions for alleviating corruption and corrupt practices during the period is done in section four, along with some proposals for eradicating same. The last section concludes the chapter.

Corruption: theoretical perspectives

The term corruption, like many social science concepts does not possess a concise and widely accepted definition. Like beauty which is often said to be in the eyes of the beholder, corruption is in the eyes of the condemner, not in those of its beneficiary. Thus, depending on what angle it is being examined from and for what purpose, it can be seen as "the act of making, or the process of becoming evil or wicked; bribery, dishonesty; it is also seen to be synonymous with rot and decay."[3]

Further, the *Lexicon Webster Dictionary* defines corruption as:

> ...the act of corrupting, or the state of being corrupt, putrefactive decomposition; putrid matter; moral perversion; depravity; perversion of integrity; corrupt or dishonest proceedings, bribery, perversion from a state of purity; debasement.

---

[3] *World Book Dictionary* (Thorndike-Barnhart and Field Enterprises Educational Corporation, London).

From these definitions, it is obvious that in the word 'corruption' lies a hint of evil. it is clear then that all that corruption does to or for any country or system plagued by it is to have negative and damaging impacts on its socio-economic and political fabric.

Heidenheimer (1978) has identified three variants of the phenomenon based on the objective they set out to achieve. These are public office centred, market centred and public interest centred corruption.[4] Public office centred corruption is seen to deal with abuse of public trust and official positions and responsibilities for self-serving objectives. Oftentimes, this would not result in monetary gains as for example, when the head of an organisation or country employs or appoints someone based on personal relationship rather than merit. When the head of an organisation or country employs or appoints someone based on personal relationship rather than merit. When public office is converted into an avenue for the maximisation of income and/or property as in the case of the Osborne Road land scandal, market-centred corruption has occurred. Public interest-centred corruption emphasises the abuse of public trust to serve cliental, cleavage, communal and other group interests as for instance, the citing of an airport by the Nigerian Airways in an obviously unviable town or route simply because it is the capital of the managing director's state of origin.

Corruption exists the world over and is therefore not a strange practice in any country - capitalist or communist, developed or developing - percolating the vertical and horizontal structures of society. Generally, it affects a society in two stages: one, a society in transition from

---

[4]   A. Heidenheimer, (ed.) *Political Corruption. Readings in Comparative Analysis*, (New Jersey, 1977), Pp. 3-30.

underdeveloped to developing often falls prey to corruption because of the urgent need of the people for individual material success. Two, is when a society is in decline or opportunities for competition are circumscribed by unfavourable socioeconomic developments.[5] In both cases, if such societies are morally lax, the danger of corruption penetrating is much easier and faster. Once this happens, remedying the system becomes a Herculean task.

These two characterizations confirm the fact that corruption is not an exclusive feature of developing countries. in developed western nations like Italy for instance, politics and politicians are characterized by a corrupt tradition of collecting bribes for patronage and the mafia who extort money to protect.[6] Socialist Party boss and former Prime Minister - Bettino Craxi - was reported to have faced more than 50 charges of alleged corruption and abuse of office. Though he denied all the charges, he resigned, quitting his more than 20 years domination of the Italian political scene amidst the deluge of businessmen testifying against him for negotiating several kickbacks from government contracts.

In Britain too, two ministers resigned amidst widespread allegations of sleaze.[7] And the Clinton administration in the US had corruption on the agenda for the December 1994 summit of the Americas in Miami, Florida.[8]

Though corruption exists the world over, it is wantonly indulged in and therefore more devastating in neo-colonial dependent capitalist countries like Nigeria. Thus, it is not

---

[5] *Newswatch*, March 9, 1992, p. 14.
[6] *African Concord,* March 8, 1993, p. 24.
[7] *Newsweek,* November 14, 1994. p. 24.
[8] Ibid., p. 11.

surprising to find all the three categories enunciated manifesting in many such countries and particularly in Nigeria, considering that corruption operates at both individual and group levels.

By the same token, the real focus on corruption, particularly now, is in the economies of the developing world and in those countries undergoing transition from communism to capitalism. The explanation for this lies among others, in the fact that being usually also politically unstable, the scale of corruption is so great that it risks causing political unrest, which like in a cycle, can have enormous impact on the reforms these countries may be undergoing.

According to Linda Chalker in an interview with *Newsweek*, 'corruption is a major impediment to development'. Thus, the fight against corruption is more serious now and in developing countries for two reasons: one, those involved in the process of economic development are becoming increasingly dissatisfied with aid and development projects being stalled by corruption. Two, austere times have made it imperative that any acts of corruption be frowned out. Since the beginning of the 1980s for instance, when most of sub-Saharan Africa has grown even poorer, the environment has become less disposed to corrupt practices. In Tanzania for an example, *New African* reports that donors who have been propping up the economy have suddenly rebelled against the huge amounts of money lost in corruption and tax evasion and have threatened to cut off all aid. President Mwinyi had earlier admitted that his government was collecting less than 20 per cent of the revenue due to it.[9]

---

[9] *New African* (London) March 1995, p. 26.

For years, economists have held the opinion that corruption is a problem of controlled economies where nothing worked without a bit of greasing the palms, saying corruption is an outgrowth of government involvement in the economy. They conclude that unnecessary and excessive government intervention reduces efficiency. This sort of intervention is coming in post-colonial societies like Nigeria. In such situations, the implication is that corruption can and may be acceptable. In the particular case of Nigeria and under the Babangida administration, this view is perfectly in order, as for instance, government through its deregulation program further opened up avenues for the practice of corruption.[10]

In many countries similar to Nigeria, government and administration account for the greatest part of the manifestations of corruption for the simple fact that leadership and the bureaucracy are the major mediums through which resources for developmental purposes are channelled.[11] In Uganda for instance, the high level of graft compelled her to invite the Berlin based international organisation - Transparency International - to fight widespread corruption in the country. Corruption is rampant not only in the traditional civil service but also in government-owned parastatals and organisations and commercial banks. In Kenya too, there are reported cases of massive thefts of public funds involving powerful and highly connected Kenyans.[12]

In Nigeria, the situation is farther the case considering the over-developed and robust constitution of the state

---

[10] As was experienced in the foreign exchange trade.

[11] S.H.C. Alatas, *Intellectuals in Developing Societies.* (London: Frank Cass, 1977).

[12] *New African, loc. cit.*, p. 27.

coupled with the prebendal character of politics in Nigeria.[13] This peculiar character is manifested among others in the spoils system and prevailing patron-client relations entrenched in community values and beliefs. Thus, for our purpose, it is plausible to define corruption as the misuse of power or (public) office by those in positions of authority or any public trust, for personal or group gain or end in whatever form - monetary or otherwise. This type of corruption was evident during the Babangida era when large scale revelations of corruption where exposed by the media in the Nigerian Telecommunications Company, the Nigerian National Petroleum Company, the Drug Enforcement Agency, the Electoral Commission and even the judiciary,[14] as well as many other organisations and sectors more in the public rather than private sectors.

However, one believes that the Nigerian problem extends far beyond and is much more complicated than a simple decision to merely scrap all government controls. Due to scarcity of goods and services and other basic necessities of life (in the particular case of bribe giving and taking to get simple government services performed), oftentimes, you can not be sure of getting the service you paid for since everyone takes bribes independently. This makes corruption much more distortionary. Thus, even if initially corruption can be justified, eventually it is harmful as it diverts revenues from the national treasury into private pockets until government goes broke and bankrupt, so, it can no longer fund the infrastructure it needs to encourage

---

[13] L. Diamond, Class, Ethnicity and Democracy in Nigeria. (London: Macmillan, 1977), R. Joseph, Democracy and Prebendal Politics in Nigeria. The Rise and Fall of Nigeria's Second Republics, (Oxford: University Press, 1986).

[14] See *African Guardian,* November 1, 1993, *Guardian,* October 18, 1993 and *Newswatch,* October 29, 1993.

investment or provide the peoples basic needs leading to popular discontent and disaffection and ultimately, political upheavals and instability.

It can be argued that the disdain for corruption is felt mainly on grounds of morality. In the special case of Nigeria, and many developing countries, it can be said that the backwardness[15] or complete lack of (positive) societal values and cultures relating to morals allows corruption to thrive. Conversely, the high level of development of these moral values and cultures in developed countries is seen to account for the reduced level of official corruption, particularly of the market and public-interest centred specie.

A systemic and structuralist postulation of corruption explains it on account of the 'inadequate and inappropriate' 'modernization' (dependent) 'development' premise on which the state bureaucracy is founded.[16] This view is shared by Onoge who contends that the nature of Nigeria's capitalism (the fact of its being in the primitive accumulation stage) creates a cultural condition of anomie which is in turn, a fertile ground for aspiring capitalists to squeeze out social surplus from pre-capitalist formations and values. Additional political factors facilitating the movement of corruption in public life arise from the alienated colonial origins of the state whereby public officials are able to manipulate ethno-cultural cleavages in society and continue to relate to the people as colonial forces of occupation.[17]

---

[15] Alatas, *op. cit.*

[16] W. O. Craf, *The Nigerian State* (London: James Curry, 1988), p. 216.

[17] O.F. Onoge, "What is to be done about Corruption in Government," paper presented at the CASS Seminar on Corruption, Port-Harcourt, December 2-4, 1993.

The neo-colonial structures and processes which gave birth to the Nigerian state facilitate 'elite hegemony' and the emergence of a bureaucracy interested only in the interests of the elites. These processes also make the economy dependent-capitalist, and the state the major source of accumulation - thus, the struggle for control for accumulation purposes and therefore corruption. Under military regimes, Bienen and Titton argue that the political and administrative contexts in which public officers, particularly civil servants operate and which gives them 'greater freedom of action...has made them more vulnerable to charges of corruption.'[18]

Corruption flourishes whenever the citizenry are politically powerless and unorganised - common characteristics of the Nigerian people, what with leadership who have been exercising power and authority by virtue of the possession of the barrel of the gun for the past 28 out of her 47 years of independence. A political mobilisation of the people toward democratic participation can act as a check against bad government and corruption by government and public officials.[19]

In Nigeria, corruption and corrupt practices exhibit themselves in day-to-day activities, yet it is almost impossible to place a hand on it due mainly to its very nature. It is a matter than cannot be freely debated without emotion. Even where it can be objectively discussed, it cannot be established (beyond reasonable doubt), let alone to published. Cases of political corruption for instance are often shrouded by those supposed or expected to

---

[18] Biemen and Fitton, In K. Panter-Brick, *Soldiers and Oil*, (London: Frank Cass 1978), P.50.

[19] Directorate For Social Mobilisation (DSM) Political Education Manual, (Abuja, 1989), pp. 17-21.

investigate and expose them as evidence the police, the media and the judiciary. Discussion has, can and will always be hindered by the regime of the day, while the lack of access to files and documents often make investigation and therefore proving and ultimately divulging to the public impossible.

In Nigeria, and as especially shown during the Babangida era, the true nature of the horrendous malpractice perpetrated by political office holders makes it imperative to conclude that the very fact of occupation of public office translates into or gives the licence to be corrupt. Such that even crusaders against corruption and related practices, upon gaining public appointment, suddenly forget what they stood for in the past. In addition, Nigerians generally have an unwritten custom of expressing or expecting an expression of gratitude in anticipation of services about to be rendered (commonly referred to as (*egunje*, settlement, kola, dash, etc.) or in gratitude for services already rendered. The problem of where to draw the line between gratification and corruption rears its head, because gratification is an important element of everyday living, particularly where competition pervades and resources are scare - both common characteristics of the Nigerian society before, during and after the regime under examination.

In Nigeria generally and particularly evident between 1985-93, no matter how despicable as a result of corruption peoples' actions are while in government, their families, relatives, friends and kinsmen and communities still welcome them back with encomiums and reward them with chieftaincy titles because of the loot they made available in the form of basic infrastructures like roads, hospitals, water etc. to the community while in office. Thus, it is common to see efforts at investigating and or punishing corrupt practices as witch-hunting especially when the accuser or whistle blower is of a different ethnic or religious group, thus introducing tribal and religious xenophobia and antagonism into an already rotten situation.

These tendencies have been explained by P.B. Ekeh in his presentation of the two publics in Africa - the primordial and civic publics.[20] According to him, the civic public has become identified with popular politics in post-colonial Africa. It is a moral having no moral linkages but rather, dialectical relationship with the private realm (of close family, kinsmen and community). The logic of the dialectic is that it is legitimate to rob the civic public in order to strengthen the primordial public, leading to inevitable tensions and confrontations between the two. Thus, corruption arises directly from the amorality of the civic public and the legitimization of the need to seize largesse from the civil in order to benefit the primordial public as seen in embezzlement of funds and solicitation and acceptance of bribes.

Corruption under the Babangida regime: case studies

The commonest presentations of corruption and corrupt practices between 1985 and 1993 can be seen in abuse of office through extra-budgetary expenditure often aimed at gaining popularity or carrying favour or support. This was exhibited at the highest levels of governance as evidence a

---

[20] P.P. Ekeh, *Colonialism and the Two Publics in Africa: A Theoretical Statement.* And Personal Communication September 1985. University of Ibadan. Nigeria.

confidential World Bank report quoted in the Financial Guardian:

> ...while the practice of spending oil revenues through dedication accounts and other devices outside the purview of statutory budgetary and accounting controls has re-emerged on a large-scale ...In addition, significant domestic currency spending appears to have occurred without any apparent budgetary authorizations...Worst of all, some $1 billion equivalent of revenues was allocated under ill-defined and poorly documented procedures outside the usual accounting framework...[21]

This fact was further made in a statement by the Chairman of the Panel on the Reform and reorganization of the Central Bank of Nigeria (CBN) - Dr. Pius Okigbo. On 'dedicated' and other special 'accounts' which the committee that was constituted by the Abacha administration was instructed to examine, it was found that they were established in 1988 to house the proceeds of the sale of crude oil dedicated to special projects and to receive the windfall oil revenues from the Gulf War. The committee revealed that between September 1988 and June 30, 1994, US$12.4 billion had been recorded in the Accounts. It found that this had been liquidated in 6 years; spent on what could neither be adjudged genuine high priority nor truly regenerative investment; that neither the President nor the CBN governor accounted to anyone for these massive extra-budgetary expenditures; that these disbursements were clandestinely undertaken while the

---

[21] *Financial Guardian,* October 18, 1993. P.3. See also *African Guardian,* November 1 1993, p. 15.

country was openly reeking with a crushing external debt overhang. The report then went ahead to recommend the immediate closure of these accounts with the outstanding balance of some $206 million paid into the external reserves.[22]

The above are clearly examples of public interest-centred type of corruption under the Babangida administration. Market-centred corruption showed in terms of the creation and payment of ghost workers; illegal oil sales and allocation of crude oil which decision was the exclusively and strictly that of the presidency;[23] and auctioning of public property ranging from cars to seized goods; fraud, forgeries and bribery. Also common were kickbacks and commissions on government projects and purchases/contracts (usually not less than 10 per cent). Contracts for one, having become one of the sad facts of our national life were further ingrained in the system under the Babangida regime as almost every government business was conducted via contracts. This enabled the people in authority to award contracts to their girlfriends, relations or political clients; or to have unearned kickbacks in kind or in cash. Contracting is still a booming business in Nigeria.

In addition, it was widely reported that under the regime, Government officials used the Bank for Credit and Commerce International (BCCI), (closed since 1991) to move vast sums of money out: of the country into personal foreign bank accounts, while senior civil servants received

---

[22] Statement by the Chairman on the Occasion of the submission of the Report of the Panel on the Reform and Reorganisation of the CBN. 1995, pp. 4 & 5.

[23] This is corroborated by the Tofa-Coomasie affair taken to court by the later. See *African Guardian,* November 1, 1993, p. 15.

handsome 'commissions' for services rendered to the bank.[24]

Nepotism and inappropriate job placements especially in positions in the banking industry which boomed during the era under review were typical examples of public office-centred corruption in Nigeria. A good example of Nepotism in action under the administration was the enthronement of an emir in Suleija, against the usual procedure (tradition and customs) and general wishes of majority of the people. The decision was later courageously overturned upon the demise of the administration by a Suleija High Court, following a suit filed by traditional kingmakers of Suleija.[25] This type of unnecessary interference was also tried with minimal success in the nation's citadels of learning through the appointment of favoured candidates into the positions of vice-chancellors.

Furthermore, the government's poor record of accountability amongst its officials was during that period, the bane of Nigeria's corporate life. A brief look at the NNPC during Dr. Chu Okongwu's tenure is useful here. Newspaper publications reported a lot of corrupt practices had been going on at the nation's biggest foreign exchange earner. The most vivid case involved a project which committed Nigeria to hire four tankers to store, in an interim arrangement, petroleum products imported through the Lagos port. The need to import these products was based on the established facts that the nation's four refineries in Port-Harcourt, Warri and Kaduna are beset with problems ranging from inefficiency to deficiency. The

---

[24] *Newsweek, op. cit.,* p. 14; *African Guardian.* November 1, 1993. pp. 12-14.
[25] This was widely reported in many Nigerian newspapers. See especially *The Guardian.*

perennial problem of fuel scarcity which was a common feature during the period under review was therefore to be addressed by importation.

Dr. Okongwu was soon succeeded by Phillip Asiodu who saw a solution slightly differently. He thought it better to buy outright rather than hire the tankers. In the process, payments for hiring were to be suspended so that arrangements for outright purchase can be processed. He could not complete this assignment when Don Etiebet took over as minister. Barely one week into office and during a one-week trip to Geneva for an OPEC meeting, payment for $41 million was made and completed for the hiring of tankers.

A number of questions easily come to mind from this whole episode regarding the propriety of acquiring foreign facilities and materials for the NNPC. Some of these include:

1. Why does the nation's biggest industry not keep any or proper records/accounts of its activities?

2. Why and how did a project which is not in the best interest of the Corporation and which does not have the best intentions for the nation get approved in the first place?

3 Relatedly, how could hiring storage tanks for imported petroleum products sound more sensible than outright purchase (of the tankers), or better still, the use of available funds to repair damaged or dysfunctional refineries?

4. How and why did suspected and involved officials of the NNPC already on suspension, suddenly get retired with full benefits when their case was still pending in court?

5. How did and can the NNPC case already in the court be withdrawn so abruptly only to be transferred to the Miscellaneous Offences Tribunal?

6. How could the reliefs sought by the accused persons' lawyers that the accused men not be re-arrested by the Police, the State Security Service (SSS), the Nigerian section of International Police (Interpol) and any other government controlled law enforcement agency, until they are ready to prosecute them before the tribunal be favoured?

Attempts to provide answers to these questions would surely expose the kind of rot and decay that pervades the NNPC among other government agencies. This was created and entrenched by the condoning of corruption.[26] Today, and two years after the incident, prosecution seems to have been quietly shelved.

Government under Babangida turned a blind eye to corruption by disregarding or trivialising it thus giving tacit support to its blossoming by not taking drastic steps to punish or make scapegoats of public officers accused of corrupt practices. The celebrated Ms Jennifer Madike/Fidelis Oyakhilome of the NDLEA case, the Peoples' Bank/Tai Solarin case, the Governor Maina of Borno State and the case of Rivers State Governor and the

---

[26] A.T. Okoosi, "Government and Corruption in Nigeria: A General Impression,' in *Annals of the Social Science Council of Nigeria,* No.5, January-December 1993, p. 115.

Alhaji Bashir/Vice-President Augustus Aikhomu case are all instances in which the administration virtually defended its officials without prior investigation. In the latter case, rather than set up a probe panel, Alhaji Bashir was locked up under Decree 2 and later let loose.

In a 1992 paper to the Nigerian Political Science Association (NPSA) in ASCON, Badagry, I wrote on an assessment of the famous Political Transition Programme (PTP) of the last administration:

> Most significant in all this is government's tacit support for corruption. Government officials are asked to ensure accountability and not necessarily not to be corrupt. These are two different but similar calls ... Instead, it (government) comes out often in defence of such officers. Hence, corruption, so trite within the present dispensation is the deal in vogue being carried out with more fanfare and pomposity. The system is further characterised by patronage, rewarding and punishing.[27]

It is the popular view that up and until 1993, President BABANGIDA did not make corruption the theme of any of his public statements. Neither did the word feature prominently in the administrations affairs. Thus, it is easy to conclude it never was an issue to the administration. Of course, a mere mention or even repeated mentioning of the word does not necessarily translate to action, as seen in the fact that with all the hew and cry about corruption by the ING, of Ernest Shonekan, he was himself among the many

---

[27] A.T. Okoosi,, "The Political Transition Programme, 19871992: An Assessment", Paper presented at the 19th Annual Conference of the Nigerian Political Science Association (NPSA), ASCON, Badagry, December 14-16, 1992.

other public officers, a shareholder in the Osborne Road land scandal.[28]

The Osborne road land scandal also needs to be espoused for not only did it have its origins in the administration of President Babangida it showed the extent to which the administration legitimised corruption. Osborne road is a private beachfront property in Lagos. It was acquired by the Federal Government through a hastily promulgated Decree No.52 of 1993 (The Lands Title Vesting etc), which confiscates and vests in the Federal Government all lands within 100 metres of Nigeria's shoreline, including all lands reclaimed from any lagoon, sea, ocean in or bordering the Federal Republic of Nigeria.

The decree came with it an ouster clause, but in the hurry to promulgate it, the administration did not seem to realise that the decree voided the provisions of the 1989 constitution which forbids the courts from inquiring into or issuing any judgement or order in respect of the subject, and declaring null and void any judgement or order which may have pre-dated the decree. Further amazing was the fact that the decree was backdated 18 whole years to January 1, 1975.[29] Obviously Decree 52 was not inspired by public interest considerations, but assuming that it was even in the public good, it challenged the Lagos State Government as:

1. it violated the Land Use Act which vests land control in state governments and in this case, the Lagos State government;

---

[28] *Guardian* October 13, 1993 and November 6, 1993.

[29] According to the Guardian reports, the Osborne Road land had already been reclaimed by a Real estate company which had also been involved in a 17-year old battle for ownership of the land.

2. it violated the rights of all those who live in the shoreline and lagoon shores of Nigeria since by virtue of the decree, they ceased to possess and were suddenly tenants who must renew or obtain leases on what they have always known to be their ancestral villages and homes.

The whole episode, a typical example of market-centred corruption was another scenario in which abuse of office and corruption was both institutionalised and displayed in its most naked form. The land was shared among a select group of the ruling elite at sharply discounted prices. Today, and probably as a result of the public outcry the issue raised, the land has been shared between the Lagos State and Federal Government, without any consideration for or consultation with the masses of the people and their ancestors who have lived there all their lives.

The last administration also encouraged corruption when it promulgated various decrees returning various properties earlier seized from some past officials including dead ones, who had property in excess of their legitimate earnings. Some of the Decrees include No.49 of 1991, No.70 of 1992 and No. 24 of 1993.[30] A last one, No. 54 of 1993 was promulgated only a few days to the administration's demise. This was in a bid to get some of the beneficiaries (semi-gods in their various regions) to canvass for public support for the administration to extend its tenure. These kinds of actions are prone to encourage public officers to disregard calls for probity and accountability in government since there exists the possibility of regaining any seized property (it may be as

---

[30] *African Concord*, March 7, 1994, P.29.

well be as well be seen as being kept in trust) in the future, depending on the mood of the government of the day. By extension, it is also possible for a public officer to corruptly enrich himself, and upon being accused, flee the country and return after a few years (to his booty) when all would have been forgotten and at times even pardoned by the state. Regarding the return of seized properties to their owners, it should be observed that some of these properties are and have been returned without consideration for the additional expenditures (to the detriment of tax-payers) that have been incurred on them whilst being forfeitures.

Lastly, the example of the situation at the still-born National Assembly as it prepared for the take-off of the presidential system of government is another instance of condonement and institutionalization of corruption. In order to establish the financial situation of the Houses of Assembly, the Senate president set up a panel to probe legislative state of accounts in December of 1992. The panel's report noted that,

> the administrative leadership of the National Assembly failed to set priorities that would have assured prudent financial resource management, efficient and effective usage of funds, and ensure accountability which would have given credit to the preparedness of the Military administration for the take-off of this most important arm of the presidential system of government.

The panel said that ₦402 million was released at various times for the operational activities of the assembly during the fiscal year 1992 and the administrative leadership expended ₦306 million on contract awards which were now being described as shady since "contracts were indiscriminately awarded, funds (were) imprudently managed and maintenance costs of new vehicles sky-rocketed without adequate control." The panel was particularly irked by the activities of the Departmental Tenders Board (DTB) which was said to have in defiance of logic and known contractual laws thrown overboard all principles governing contract awards. Some of these actions included by-passing the DTB's secretary, advance payment up to the tune of 75 per cent of contract sum, most of which was paid before (the) project take-off date and so on.[31]

Even though the Presidency was reported to have summoned the director-general of the National Assembly, he responded promptly and had a good explanation in the sense that his books were balanced and seemingly against the initially approved expenditure heads.[32] In Nigeria however, this does not mean much, especially when we consider that securing a receipt for anything has never been a hurdle too high to scale. The administration by not dealing appropriately and decisively, once again shied away from what should normally be the responsibility of a good government.

Critique of government provisions for dealing with corruption during the Babangida era: suggestions for a saner polity

From the above and especially the case studies put forward in the preceding pages, it is clear that no aspect of National

---

[31] *African Concord,* March 8, 1993, p. 13.
[32] Ibid., p. 17.

life was not touched by the stench of corruption in various forms) that characterised the Babangida administration between 1985 and 1993, yet it had legal provisions for dealing with the problem.

According to Section 11 (1) of Part 1 of the fifth schedule of the 1979 Constitution,

> Every public officer shall within 3 months after the coming into force of this code of conduct or immediately after taking office and thereafter - (a) at the end of every four office; submit to the Code of Conduct Bureau a written declaration of all his properties, assets and liabilities and those of his spouse, or unmarried children under the age of 21 years.[33]

The affected public officers include the president and his vice, all members and officers of Parliament, state governors and their deputies, all judicial officers and staff of courts of law, ministers and commissioners, all members of the armed forces and the police, all persons in the civil service, all officers of Nigerian foreign missions, chairmen and staff of local government councils, chairmen and members of boards as well as staff of government corporations, all staff of federal or state universities and other academic institutions, chairmen, members and staff of permanent commissions or councils.

The constitution provided for a Code of Conduct Tribunal to try officers found to have breached the code and the punishment was 'vacation of office or seat in any legislative house as the case may be; disqualification from the membership of a legislative house and from holding any public office for a period not exceeding 10 years; and

---

[33] *African Concord* March 8, 1993, pp. 12-17.

seizure and forfeiture to the state of any property acquired in abuse or corruption of office."

The procedure of assets declaration involved a public officer filling an assets declaration form to be served him/her by the Bureau and swearing to an oath before a High Court Judge and then returning same, all within 30 days to the Bureau.

Following the military coup of December 1983, the Buhari regime suspended the constitution, disbanded the Code of Conduct Bureau and transferred its functions to the Nigerian Security Organisation (NSO). The General Babangida administration reversed the situation four years after it came to power in 1989. It promulgated the Code of Conduct Bureau and Tribunal decree and reinstated all the original Provisions of the Bureau in the Constitution as well as its chairman. Further, a five-man Code of Conduct Tribunal was inaugurated. And this was where it ended, with corruption rather than reduces blossom instead.

The above provisions and institutions were inadequate for they did not curb corruption during the regime's life. For one, the benefit that the Nigerian state would have derived from this statutory obligation of public office holders remained elusive and illusory. This was for the simple reason that such declarations, if and when made at all, are among the most closely guarded state secrets through the Code of Conduct Bureau as its agency. Thus, it was and has not been possible for any former public office holder to find himself in a position where he is required to not only declare his assets, but to justify his legitimate entitlement to them.

Two, the provisions dealt only with material corruption which the laws may be able to deal with. However, another common but difficult to substantiate form of corruption which also characterised the period under review was moral corruption a difficult and most pernicious corruption. Corruption is not restricted to money or gifts. As indicated earlier it also entails any undue influence exerted in pursuit of any special interests. This is so because such influence bends the rules and the system to serve those interests.

Three there were, no clear steps, apart from verbal threats, to be taken when a public officer does not complete, swear to and submit an assets declaration form at the beginning and end of his service. Four, during the era under review, there were many situations well-known to the public, of public officers acquiring property in excess of their legitimate income in the name of their trusted family members friends or kinsmen, raising the issue of authentication. Five, regular courts rather than tribunals would have been better avenues of establishing innocence or guilt of those arraigned for offences related to asset declaration. Finally, even where public officers had been found guilty of contravening the stipulated provisions, no decisive punitive actions were taken against erring officers under the regime.

Even though Achebe has said that "corruption in Nigeria has passed the alarming and entered the fatal stage, and Nigeria will die if we keep pretending that she is only slightly indisposed,"[34] I, unlike many who have lost hope in the country, believe that the Nigerian situation is not (yet) beyond redemption (the discouraging activities of subsequent administrations notwithstanding). There is still some hope for Nigeria, based on the consideration or utilisation of the defence of development economists that, 'Australia was settled by convicts and rapaciously corrupt

---

[34] *Sunday Punch* April 17, 1994, pp. 5 & 6

British officials, yet within two generations, was law abiding and prosperous.'[35]

How then do we deal with corruption in order that our hope can be realised? First, a decongestion of Nigeria's attractive federal centre which is so amenable to and fertile for the very and corruption is of priority importance. However, not only should government control be reduced, but better wages, provision and availability of basic needs and amenities fro bureaucrats and citizens generally is important. This is in the hope that when these are readily available, the urge for personal aggrandizement to satisfy these needs will reduce. This of course does not stop the greedy, kleptomaniac and materialistic from engaging in corrupt practices.

Committed whistle blowers in the press and judiciary need to be encouraged and protected by society to continue in such duty no matter the risks. Along side this is an urgent need for societal re-orientation and re-socialisation for awareness about corruption and to encourage a general sense of civic virtue which would of course usually take a long time.

Finally, one cannot but agree with General Obasanjo's opinion that the development of a tradition of local grassroots democracy and the emplacement of a democratic government may help by ensuring the existence of laws and institutions which effectively discourage and punish corruption.[36] This means that until Nigeria evolves a good leadership and government, efforts at curbing corruption will be fruitless.[37] This point returns us to the fact that

[35] C. Achebe, *The Trouble with Nigeria*.

[36] *Newsweek, op. cit.*, p. 14.

[37] Ibid.

curbing corruption in government is a first step to sanitizing the whole society.

Conclusion

It is clear from all the above that what may have begun as an illegality gradually advanced into a social process under the Babangida regime. The rot and decay set in, largely inordinately and uncontrollably, and which if not quickly arrested will grow even bigger and with horrific consequences. The inextricable connection between government, politics and corruption was very visible under the Babangida regime when corruption was elevated to the status of an instrument of state policy. Unfortunately, the kind of strong centre (made even stronger during the administration in terms of control of resources) that Nigeria operates unconsciously incubated the vice. Furthermore, the harsh and biting economic situation that characterised the period 1985-1993, as a result of the economic policies in the form of structural adjustment programme (SAP), had negative consequences for the generality of Nigerians. This made their domination in an environment characterized by, on the one hand, abject poverty and, on the other, very prone to materialism, very easy for the government of the day.

Malthouse Monographs on Africa

Editor: Dafe Otobo, DPhil (Oxford),
Professor, University of Lagos, Lagos, Nigeria

Advisory Editorial Board

Professor Adele Jinadu, Centre for Advanced Social Science, Port Harcourt, Nigeria.
Professor John Ohiorhenuan, UNDP, New York, USA
Professor Eddie Webster, University of Witwatersrand, Johannesburg, South Africa
Gavin Williams, St Peter's College, University of Oxford, UK.

Malthouse Monographs on Africa

Malthouse Monographs on Africa are peer-reviewed works on Africa covering the six main areas of a) social sciences and development studies; b) history, law and international relations; c) environmental and agricultural studies; d) gender, refugee and conflict studies; e) strategic and defence studies; and f) labour and trades unions.

The Monographs are intended to provide an arena for free contestation of ideas and as outlet for research and empirical studies on Africa in the areas indicated above. The monographs thus have no links with, nor funded by, any African government or political party. Nor do the views expressed in them represent those of the editorial board.

Works for consideration may be of purely theoretical, or historical or applied in nature or policy-oriented. Such may be sent directly to the Series Editor as electronic files (dafeotobo2002@yahoo.co.uk) in Microsoft Word Rich Text format, or to the publishers (malthouse_press@yahoo.com}. Diskettes and hardcopies may also be sent to the publishers at the address on the imprint page. The aim is to publish accepted works within three months.

Malthouse Monographs on Africa
Volumes 1 – 9

Guest Series Editor: Dayo Oluyemi-Kusa,
Director, External Conflict Prevention & Resolution,
Institute for Peace and Conflict Resolution, The Presidency,
Abuja, Nigeria

- Rotimi T. Suberu, *Institutional structure and process of government in Nigeria, 1985-1993*
- R. A. Akindele, *Federalism under General Babangida's administration in Nigeria*
- Dele Olowu & Kunle Awotokun, *Local government and the IBB administration*
- Cyril Obi, *The Nigerian private sector under adjustment and crisis 1985-1993*
- Bola A. Akinterinwa, *General Ibrahim Babangida's legacy: the domestic and international dimensions*
- Nereus I. Nwosu, *Nigeria's foreign policy under General Babangida*
- Antonia T. Oko-Osi, *Corruption and corrupt practices: institutionalization and legitimation under the Babangida Administration*
- Oyeleye Oyediran & Babafemi Badejo, *The military and democracy in Nigeria: the Political Bureau Report*
- Adekunle Amuwo, *Politics of the annulment of June 12 presidential election in Nigeria*

Malthouse Press Limited
43 Onitana Street, Off Stadium Hotel Road,
Surulere, Lagos, Lagos State
E-mail: malthouse_press@yahoo.com
malthouse_lagos@yahoo.co.uk
Tel: +234 (01) -773 53 44; 0802 364 2402

All rights reserved. No part of this publication may be reproduced,
transmitted, transcribed, stored in a retrieval system or translated into any
language or computer language, in any form or by any means, electronic,
mechanical, magnetic, chemical, thermal, manual or otherwise, without the
prior consent in writing of Malthouse Press Limited, Lagos, Nigeria.

This book is sold subject to the condition that it shall not by way of trade,
or otherwise, be lent, re-sold, hired out, or otherwise circulated without the
publisher's prior consent in writing, in any form of binding or cover other than
in which it is published and without a similar condition, including this
condition, being imposed on the subsequent purchaser.

© Malthouse Monographs on Africa 2007
First Published 2007
ISBN 978 023 232 X

Distributors:
African Books Collective Ltd
Email: abc@africanbookscollective.com
Website: http://www.africanbookscollective.com

Guest Editor's comment

All the Monographs in this series attempt to explore and document events, policies and impact of the General Ibrahim Babangida-led military regime in Nigeria, covering the period 1985 to 1993. These contributions were originally for a book edited by me on that regime but other considerations, especially that of comprehensiveness of coverage of arguably the most momentous phase in Nigeria's post-Civil War socio-political development, led to the shelving of that idea. It was thought that a more useful scope or coverage might be achieved through a continuing development of Monographs on different facets of Nigerian society under this regime – a feat which may only be possible in a book so voluminous and whose cost might be such as to be out of the reach of the intended audience.

I should like to thank all the contributors who have waited this long to see their work in print, a fate that is unlikely to befall the contributors of the other titles currently in preparation. I am grateful to the publishers for including these titles in Malthouse Monographs for Africa family.

Dayo Oluyemi-Kusa

The military and democracy in Nigeria: the Political Bureau Report

Oyeleye Oyediran
Retired Professor of Political Science, University of Lagos
&
Babafemi Badejo, PhD
Head of Political Affairs for the UN Mission in Liberia

No. 8

Contents

Introduction

One of the most popular positions taken by modernisation theorists is that the crisis of governance going on in most Third World countries of Asia, Africa and Latin America is the crisis of development. That crisis, it is argued, marks the conflict between traditionality and modernity which in the long run will usher in the modern or precisely Western values conducive to political development. Hence, to know whether or not a political system is developing is to know how it is coping with the problems of capability, reproductions, redistribution and equality.

Of those who disagree with this position, Huntington takes a front-line place. To him what is happening in most of the Third World countries is not a crisis of development or political development but political decay, and what is required is a coherent and organised leadership that will bring stability.

Whether the issue is stability or political development some argue that, in Africa in particular, the military is the most capable public institution to stem political decay. Some of the qualities of that institution which lend support to this position, it is claimed, are the decisiveness and goal-oriented nature of the men and women who lead the institution; that the institution has organisational capabilities for undertaking large-scale projects and that it has the capacity to mobilise society and its resources in support of development objectives. All these, as some military leaders in Africa have shown, are not necessarily correct. One of Ghana's former military leaders has shown this to be the case. As he puts it, "My view is that although rank, hierarchy and command which are designed for war condition, work well in barracks, they seem to break down when applied to civil administration by the military."[38] This is so, he contends, because members of the military junta frequently split due to differences of rank, personal or ethnic interest, the absence of political party ideologies or leadership loyalties. He argues that it is only where well-defined public interest constitutes the overriding concern that a military junta is able and willing to compromise and work together as a team. This, he added, is rare. Other impediments in the way of the military to be able to handle political development or political stability have been analysed elsewhere by Oyediran.[39]

In recent years, military leaders who became political leaders by staging coups have been forced by the prevailing world demand for democracy and respect for human rights to attempt transition from authoritarian rule. In both Togo and Zaire not much appears to be visible that can be called progress. In Nigeria on the other hand, the facade of progress was propagated. Not only did the military leadership prepare to hand-over to civilian administration it also claimed to prepare the country for a democratic system of government better than any that Nigerians had ever experienced. Our position in this monograph is that while General Ibrahim Babangida's military administration pretended in its rhetoric to lay a firm foundation for stability and democracy, its actions and policy decisions were serious impediments to achieving this objective. The response of the administration to the report of its own

---

[38] J.J. Rawlings.

[39] Oyeleye Oyediran and Adigun Agbaje, "Two Partyism and Democracy Transition in Nigerian," *The Journal of Modern African Studies*, vol. 29, no. 2, 1991.

Political Bureau was an important case in point. Many analysts believe that the Bureau Report provided the political transition programme for the regime.

General Babangida, many years out of office continues to maintain his position of 1987 that Nigerians and posterity be the judge of the achievements of his administration. This monograph is an attempt to do just that with respect to his effort at soliciting the views of Nigerians on his political engineering.

General Babangida and the democratic challenge

When General Babangida came to power in August 1985 Nigeria was facing serious economic problems. Hence from the 1985 debate over whether or not Nigeria should accept the offer of a huge loan from the International Monetary Fund (IMF) with all its 'conditionalities', it became clear to the new military junta that the economic crisis had two dimensions - inefficient domestic financial system and the sensitivity of the Nigerian economy to external manipulations.

While the previous military administration of General Muhammed Buhari attempted to solve the economic problem and servicing the external debt, it was marked and delegitimized by its failure to consider any programme for returning the country to a democratically elected leadership, Addressing the Nigerian Political Science Association (NPSA) in 1985, Major General Tunde Idiagbon, second-in-command in that administration, argued that they could not afford to have a political transition programme in the midst of the serious economic problems facing Nigeria. General Babangida on the other hand indicated from the very moment of seizing power in August 1985, his intention to launch a political transition programme. In his budget speech of December 31, 1985 he promised that "1986 would be marked by a search for a new political system" and announced that the country's "Armed Forces Ruling Council (AFRC)...has decided to sponsor a national debate to address... fundamental issues: smooth transition from a military to a participatory political system and a debate that would break ideas and concepts that are firmly rooted in Nigeria's social and political experience."

He went on:

> To avoid the mistakes of the past, we must aim at establishing a political system capable of ensuring justice; opportunity for the people to participate in the decision-making process and new social and economic order based on peace, stability and harmony and an equitable distribution of national resources and opportunities.[40]

Towards this end Babangida inaugurated a Political Bureau of seventeen members on January 13, 1986 and challenged it to search for "a new political order" for Nigeria. This new political order was meant "as the launching pad for the New Nigeria: prosperous, humanist and stable at home. A nation that possesses real capability in the African context and that commands and compels respect in international affairs." In his address inaugurating the Bureau, Babangida articulated the momentous 'terms of reference' for the work of the Bureau:

---

[40] 1985 Budget Speech

a) Review Nigeria's political history and identify the basic problems which have led to our failure in the past and suggest ways of resolving or coping with these problems;

b) Identify a basic philosophy of government which will determine goals and serve as a guide to the activities of governments;

c) Collect relevant information and date for the Government as well as identify other political problems that may arise from the debate;

d) Gather, collate and evaluate the contributions of Nigerians to the search for a viable political future and provide guidelines for the attainment of the consensus objective;

e) Deliberate on other political problems as may be referred to it from time to time.[41]

After the inauguration, the Bureau members had series of meetings in Abuja and Lagos reviewing and analysing the President's 1986 Budget speech and the five 'terms of reference'.

The Political Bureau was composed predominantly of intellectuals. The chairman, Samuel J. Cookey, was at the time of his selection, Pro-Chancellor and Chairman of the Council of the University of Benin. A seasoned former civil servant and educationalist, he had also held prominent appointments with UNESCO over the years. Of the other sixteen members, nine were at the time university lecturers or Professors. Five of them in political science, while a tenth, Eme Awa (also a political scientist) was at the

---

[41] *Political Bureau Report*

Nigerian Institute for Policy and Strategic Studies in Kuru. Two others were journalists, Edwin Madunagu of the *Guardian* and Haroun Adamu, managing director of the *Punch* (also trained as a political scientist), while a thirteenth, Dr. Ola Balogun, was a prominent filmmaker and writer. Two of the remaining three members were officials of the Nigerian Labour Congress (NLC), including Pascal Bafyau, then general secretary of the Nigerian Union of Railwaymen who became President of the NLC in 1989. Two of the members, Dr. (Mrs.) Rahmatu Abdullahi and Mrs Hilda Adefarasin, were women. Balogun resigned and Madunagu was eased out (through ostracism) by other members from the Bureau during 1986, leaving a total of 15 members who signed the final report.

Subsequently the members of the Bureau identified their task as:

(a) Stimulating, co-ordinating and guiding the national political debate through;

(i) organising grassroots participation and mobilising the broad masses of the people in the quest for new political order;

(ii) encouraging the contributions of professional, academics economic and social groups and organisations, and

(iii) seeking the views of men of experience in public affairs;

(b) Collecting all relevant data for the work of the Bureau and for possible use by the government;

(c) Collating, analysing and summarising the views expressed in the course of the national political debate;

(d) Reviewing Nigeria's political history and identifying the basic problems therein and making recommendations for resolving and coping with these problems;

(e) Working out a basic philosophy of government for Nigeria;

(f) Preparing a blueprint for a future political model or models for the country;

(g) Providing guidelines for the implementation of the recommended model;

(h) Providing a blueprint for an economic model consistent with the political order;

(i) Providing a time-sequence for political transition by 1990; and

(j) Deliberate on any other political matters that may be referred to the Bureau by the government.

Next, the Political Bureau members worked out 'Guidelines for the Debate', to serve as the parameters for the contribution of Nigerians to the debate. To ensure the widest possible consultations, exchange of views and participation of Nigerians, the Bureau outlined various modalities and measures. These included making the local government area the basic unit for the whole debate, guaranteeing adequate participation by the grassroots; and inviting individuals, groups and organisations to send memoranda, contribute newspaper articles as well as participate in radio and television discussions so as to mobilise the general public to participate in the debate. Altogether the Bureau received 27,324 contributions from individuals and groups, including almost 15,000 memoranda, almost 4,000 newspaper articles, 1723 recorded cassettes and video tapes, 2,214 papers in debates and conferences, 3,729 summaries of debates and interviews and 703 contribution made at public hearings organised by the Bureau.[42]

Nigeria prior to the Political Bureau: the enigma of a country

In the previous sections we have tried to present the conditions that led to the setting up of the Political Bureau. At this stage we shall try to place the circumstances surrounding the political debate in historical context to reflect the societal conditions.

To start with, it is worth noting that the political debate of 1986, organised by the Political Bureau was not the first in the history of the country. Nigerians have been confronted with an unfinished debate of this nature during the immediate past regime of General Buhari. The debate then centred on the "National Question". It was difficult then to arrive at a consensus on a number of issues such as "who are dominating whom?" "How should federal character be applied?" and "who are the educationally disadvantaged?" This debate, which the Buhari administration halted prematurely but automatically returned in full swing in Abuja later where one conference participant, Professor Obaro Ikime, noted that some of the British colonial policies had created a good number of the problems that today make Nigeria anything but a nation-state. He gave as one example, western education, which the British introduced in the south and did not in the north.

He went on:

---

[42] *Political Bureau Report.*

When it came to appointments to federal institutions, persons from the North were not required to possess the educational qualifications and experience demanded from persons from the South seeking the same positions. In that sense, it became a distinct advantage to be educationally disadvantaged... many northerners took advantage of this accommodation to rise rapidly to leading positions in public life.[43]

Ikime argued that the situation remained that way several years after independence because the group interest of the northern elite compelled it to maintain the status quo; and because the northern elite preferred to institutionalise educational backwardness and to demand concessions which helped the political dominance they enjoy.

Despite the creation of many states out of the old Northern Nigeria the idea of "One North One People" propagated by the Northern Peoples Congress (NPC) was kept alive. This was what led to the adoption of an educational policy that classified the states into the so-called educationally advantaged areas and educationally disadvantaged areas. A certain percentage of admissions into federal educational institutions are reserved for the educationally disadvantaged states.

What is generally referred to as the National Question is far from being resolved after almost five decades of independence. A long while before returning to head the Nigerian State, General Olusegun Obasanjo suggested that this was so because "ethnic chauvinism, personal aggrandisement and insensitivity to the feelings and needs of the general populace" was rampant particularly among

---

[43] *Groundwork of Nigerian History*, Heinemann, Ibadan, 1980.

the elite. He therefore called for a serious effort at national integration.

The debate which the Political Bureau initiated was in a sense a continuation of an old debate. In some circles it was regarded as an attempt by the Babangida administration to keep the nation busy while the administration got on with its task of governing as it pleased. There was a sense in which this was correct, for it was well known that certain measures and policy decisions were taken by government which made more difficult the task assigned to the Political Bureau.

One example was the proscription of the National Association of Nigerian Students (NANS) in 1986. How could the nation be expected to talk seriously and freely about national issues when some of its critical, vocal, national organs were banned? The Political Bureau protested to government on this without success. The late Chief Obafemi Awolowo and General Obasanjo, both declined to make their views known on the issues raised by the Political Bureau because they expected nothing to come out of the work of the Bureau. It was rumoured that even the Head of State, General Babangida, made it known to some retired military leaders that the exercise embarked upon by the Bureau was not meant to be taken seriously.

With the benefit of hindsight, the Political Bureau may seem to have been just one of the populist designs of the Babangida administration, in the same way as the issue of the loan from the international Monetary Fund (IMF) was put to the nation for debate. It must be added, however, that despite the suspicion of many members of the Political Bureau that they were probably being sent on a fruitless mission, every member of the group ignored this and worked hard to produce a report that history will judge to be a serious attempt to chart a new path for Nigeria.

The importance of the Political Bureau's mission was perhaps signalled in the controversy shortly following its submission. When the *Newswatch* devoted its April 13, 1987 issue entirely to the report, quoting extensively from it before government reacted, the magazines premises were sealed off and the publication banned for six months. To interpret this to mean that government took the Report seriously would be a mistake.

However, between 1987 and 1993, the Babangida administration repeatedly sought to legitimize its new or changed policies with quotations, often incorrect or misleading, from the Political Bureau Report.

Government's reaction to the Report

It is interesting to note that the Political Bureau did not provide a summary either of its report or its recommendations. As its chairman Dr. J.S. Cookey pointed out in his speech at the presentation ceremony, this was to induce those who would advise government to read the report and all the recommendations in their entirely. Space does not permit us to review here, government's reaction on every issue and recommendation. Selecting the most important issues, we deal first with what government rejected completely and then with areas in which government accepted the Bureau's recommendations.

One of the most important aspects of the Report was the Bureau's call for a new philosophy of government in Nigeria. Its recommendation that Nigeria should adopt a socialist socio-economic system, in which the state was committed to the nationalisation and socialisation of the commanding heights of the national economy was flatly rejected by government which claimed the introduction of any philosophy or political ideology would be an imposition on the nation. Ideology in government's view, would evolve with time and political maturity. Instead of an ideology, government felt satisfied with the goals set in the Second Development Plan of 1970-74: (a) a united, strong and self-reliant nation; (b) a great and dynamic economy; (c) a just and egalitarian society; (d) a land of bright and full opportunities for all citizens; (e) a free and democratic society. These became the "new social order" or the "new philosophy of government".

It was the position of the Political Bureau that recommending a change from the neo-capitalist to a socialist philosophy of government necessitated a new political orientation. This, it was recommended must emphasize public enlightenment, education and mass mobilisation towards the goals and objectives of the state. Specific institutions were listed as agents of social mobilisation of the entire nation, such as co-operative unions, women's organisations, youth and student's organisations, age grades, village and clan councils. These, the Bureau argued should be institutionalised, democratised and given specific functions to perform in the political system. The Bureau therefore called for the initiation of a co-ordinated, comprehensive, coherent and sustained programme of social mobilisation and political education for Nigeria.

Though the government rejected the recommended political philosophy it accepted the need for social and political mobilisation of the people. The government preferred, however, the name National Directorate of

Social Mobilisation (dropping the additional designation "and Political Education" suggested by the Bureau).

Critics of the government on its rejection of the recommended political philosophy concentrated their attention on what appeared as an illogical position of government. How can government reject the new philosophy, they asked, yet accept the operational pillar on which its success was hung? Over time it became clear that what government had accepted was not the type of social mobilisation called for by the Political Bureau but a diffuse institution meant to do nothing different from the existing propaganda machines of government. It was little wonder, then, that after five years of existing 1987-92, and with nothing to show for it, government decided to merge the Directorate of Social Mobilisation with the existing Ministry of Information.[44]

---

[44]   Adigun Agbaje who monitored the National Directorate's activities commented on the mobilisation effort of the Babangida administration. He said:

> the Babangida administration's attempt at a planned mobilisation toward the so-called new political culture where 'new' implies 'better,' and 'pro-democratic' and 'developmentalist' never really took off fully. In fact, following the emergence of elected party leadership in 1990, even its major instrument of policy formulation in this regard, the Directorate of Social Mobilisation, fell under the shadow of partisan suspicions as the new leadership of the NRC were quick to accuse the Directorate's top leadership of having pro-SDP tendencies.

See his "Mobilisation for a New Political Culture" in Larry Diamond, Anthony Kirk-Greene and Oyeleye Oyediran (eds), *Democratic Transition in Nigeria: Politics, Governance and Civil society, 1986-1993*, Ibadan: Vantage Press (1994). On mobilisation efforts

One final area in which the government flatly rejected the Bureau's recommendation was in the political and constitutional system. The Bureau recommended a unicameral legislature at both the state and federal levels, strongly emphasising the need to cut the cost of government. In addition it recommended that representation in the legislature be on the basis of territory rather than population or functional or interest group. The government instead re-emphasised the position as contained in the 1979 Constitution that the principle of representation on the basis of equality of states at the upper chamber and on population at the lower chamber will continue.

Nonetheless, there were several important areas in which government did accept the Bureau's recommendation. Probably the most important of these concerns state and local government. We can state categorically that the Bureau almost broke up on the issue of creation of more states in Nigeria.[45] After a long, tedious, and often emotional debate which lasted several weeks, it was decided that, since the Bureau was equally divided the chairman did not vote on this and most issues, though his position was known to members, the two

generally, see also, Agbaje's "Political Education and Public Policy in Nigeria: The War Against Indiscipline (WAI)," *Journal of Commonwealth and Comparative Studies*, vol. XXVII, no. 1 (March 1988); "Travails of the Secular state: Religion, Politics and the Outlook on Nigeria's Third Republic," *Journal of Commonwealth and Comparative Studies*, vol. XXVII, 3, Nov. 1990. Also see Eghosa Osaghae, "The Character of the State, Legitimacy, Crisis and social Mobilisation in *Africa Development*, vol. XIV, no. 2 (1989), pp. 27-47 and Peter Koehn, "Competitive Transition to Civilian Rule: Nigeria's First and second Experiment's", *The Journal of Modern African Studies*, vol. 27, no. 2, 1989, pp. 426 ff.

[45] Oyediran was a member of the Political Bureau.

positions should be put to government in the Report. One group saw the creation of more states as no panacea to fundamental problems facing the nation; the other saw the creation of more states as a way of establishing "an organic federalism" and enhancing political stability, by removing a major source of tension. Paragraph 10-058 of the Report, states:

> In assessing the... views and proposals from the Nigerian people on the issue of state creation, the Bureau is unanimous in rejecting suggestions to either abolish or merge some of the existing states. Opinion in the Bureau is, however, divided between support for retaining the existing nineteen-state structure and creating a few additional ones, the numbers or states ranging from two to six. We present the contending positions in full below to assist government in disposing of this matter in the larger interest of the country and the success of the new social order proposed in this report.

It was most regrettable that those who prepared the government's position should claim, as they did, in the White Paper that the Political Bureau recommended the creation of additional states in Nigeria. To be charitable, we want to suggest that those who prepared government's position did not read the whole of the presentation in Chapter X of the Report, in particular all the paragraphs dealing with creation of states. Otherwise if they read them and still concluded that the Bureau recommended the creation of additional states, they were guilty of having deceived both the government and the Nigerian people. It was on the basis of this wrong conclusion from its own review committee (headed by Major General Paul Omu) that government accepted "in principle, the creation of more states" in its White Paper.[46]

On local government, the Bureau recommended (a) that the existing 301 multi-purpose local government areas be retained and a maximum of five development area councils be created in each local government area; (b) that village and neighbourhood committees be created in each development council area and that specific responsibilities be delegated to them as well as village or neighbourhood committees; (c) that local government share of the Federation Account be not less than twenty per cent and that states should contribute ten per cent of their internally generated revenue to Local Government Joint Account. These recommendations were generally accepted by the government.

On the issue of political party system, four positions were canvassed and noted in the Bureau's report. These were (a) no party or zero party; (b) single party; (c) two party and (d) multiparty systems. The Bureau recommended the adoption of a two-party system, rejected the no-party system, offering the following rationale for a party-system:

> Political parties can be seen as both the expression and management of conflict within a political system. They are to be seen not only as products of their environment but also as instruments or institutions organised to affect the environment.

---

[46] It is interesting to note that the recommendation of those opposed to the creation of additional states comes before the other position in the Report. For an analysis of the struggle for new states since 1976, see Rotimi Suberu, "The Struggle for New States in Nigeria, 1976-1990," *African Affairs*, 1991, 90, pp. 499-522.

Viewed this way, political parties function as agents
of political participation and political mobilisation.

The Bureau also rejected the one-party system as
"inherently dictatorial" and the multiparty system as too
chaotic. It therefore settled on the limited degree of
regimentation of a two-party system, but it added that the
two-party system should function under conditions which
ensured that:

(a) both political parties accept the national
philosophy of government;
(b) the differences between the two political parties
are the priorities and strategies of
implementation of the national objectives;
(c) membership of the political parties be open to
every citizen of Nigeria irrespective of place of
origin, sex, religion or ethnic grouping;
(d) the national executive organ and the principal
officers of each political party reflect the federal
character of Nigeria;
(e) each of the political parties be firmly established
in at least two-thirds of the local government
areas in each of the states including the Federal
Capital Territory (Abuja).

Finally on this issue, the Bureau recommended that the
two political parties be funded substantially by the government and that additional funds be raised by the political
parties from registration fees, annual dues and sale of party
emblems. All these recommendations were accepted by the
government in its White Paper.

Ultimately, however, the government action on each of
these issues did not necessarily correspond with its
declarations and intentions as published in the White Paper

on the Political Bureau Report. It is to these actions that we now turn.

Government action

The committee that deliberated on the Political Bureau report and made recommendations to the government was headed by a member of the Armed Forces Ruling Council and the highest decision-making body of the regime until its transformation in 1992 to the National Defence and Security Council (NDSC). Whether misled by its review Committee or not, government announced the creation of two additional states - Akwa Ibom and Katsina soon after the Report was released to the public. General Babangida stated his reason as follows:

> This Administration wishes to emphasise that no further comments or petition either by self-seeking political aspirants or champions of communal or ethnic groups will be tolerated on this matter during the period of transition, For this Administration, the number of states in Nigeria shall remain twenty-one.[47]

This was generally accepted by the Nigerian people, as in some way, it provided an answer to a constitutional problem which had faced the nation in 1979. Part of the requirement for a candidate to be declared winner of the presidential election was that he obtained at least one quarter of the votes cast in two-thirds of the states constituting the federation. The question of what constitutes two-thirds of nineteen states $12\frac{2}{3}$ or 13 almost derailed the

---

[47] *White Paper* on the Report of the Political Bureau.

Second Republic before it began in 1979. Making Nigeria a federation of 21 states removed that mathematical problem.

Despite his firm claim to have laid the issue to rest, two years after the creation of the two states General Babangida announced the creation of an additional nine states, making Nigeria a federation of thirty states. During the closing months of the administrations a very strong rumour circulated that still more states would be created. What was the rationale for all these new states? On every occasion that the administration made changes in the constitution or structure of government, it claimed the Political Bureau report as its source of strength. Often this constituted a minority position on some issues debated by the Bureau, whether that minority was one, two or three. For example, only one member felt very strongly that the Bureau should recommend the adoption of a one-party system for Nigeria. Only two members recommended extending the hand-over date from 1990 to 1992 and this was justification enough for the government to accept this minority view.

However, on the issue of state creation, no member recommended anything more than six additional states. Yet, altogether the Babangida administration created eleven additional states. It is our considered view that the consequence of this action was not the strengthening of the federal system. Rather it made the centre unnecessarily more powerful at the expense of the states and local governments. We accept that there is no magic number of states for a "balanced federation" but as the group that advocated the retention of the 19-state structure emphasized: "The creation of more states could lead to reopening the Pandora's box" and that "the factors and sentiments which underlie the clamour for state creation would endure unless tackled realistically" whatever the number of additional states created. The fact that more requests for state creation are still on the agenda of various groups emphasises this point.

In addition, the issue of creation of additional states as handled by the Babangida administration showed inconsistency in government policy decisions.[48] This inconsistency became a trade-mark of that administration towards the end of its life. What started as political shrewdness appeared by the end as gross cynicism and opportunism. This inconsistency became known first to the keen watchers of the administration; before long, the whole nation was aware of it. Many of these keen watchers did not speak out early. Some were "settled" to use a local concept made popular by the administration - that is, they were given "handsome purse" to enjoy the comfort that money can provide or flown abroad (sometimes it was their dependants) with generous financial assistance, for one medical problem or the other. This type of "co-optation" worked for a while, but by the fifth year of the life of the administration it could no longer be contained. It was not that the co-opted men and women talked, it was that the administration overplayed its cards. Not only was the government changing its mind on many policy issues already announced, even the most basic of questions, the transition date, was changed repeatedly first from 1990 to 1992, then to January 1993 and then to August 1993. Finally groups were sponsored to campaign for Babangida to remain in

---

[48] Some defenders of the administration saw this as political sensitivity or responsiveness. Babangida himself said toward the close of his administration "Although the administration reversed itself on some occasions in the light of articulated, superior positions, its resolute stance on... issues was based on its conviction on such issues." *The Guardian,* Saturday May 29 1993, p. 2.

power after that date. All of this raised serious questions about the integrity of the administration managing the transition. As Obasanjo puts it then, "What we have had... is manipulation on a scale almost beyond belief and rationalization of the most absurd kind."[49]

He continued:

> In the name of political engineering, the country has been converted to a political laboratory for trying out all kinds of silly experiments and gimmicks. Principle has been abandoned for expediency. All kinds of booby-traps were instituted into the transition process. The result is the crisis we now have.[50]

The crisis of confidence got so bad that despite the announcement at every available opportunity that the administration would hand-over power on August 27, 1993, the overwhelming majority of Nigerians did not believe it. Even after the government advertised in most dailies that it would indeed hand over on the appointed date, Nigerians still did not believe it. Reflecting on this situation, Obasanjo noted: "it has now got to a stage that when government says good morning, people will look out four times to ascertain the time of the day before they reply."[51]

If the Babangida administration did indeed introduce a new social order to Nigeria, it was the complete opposite of

---

[49] Text of the Proposed Speech by General Olusegun Obasanjo at the National-Council of States Meeting called by General Ibrahim Babangida, 14th November 1992.

[50] Ibid. See also Bayo Adekanye, "Thoughts on National Question," *The Guardian*, Friday and Saturday October 16 and 17, 1992.

[51] IBB, Nigeria's Greatest Problem," *Tell*, April 26, 1993. This weekly magazine devoted most of this issue to an interview given to it by General Obasanjo.

the type of social order promised and expected by Nigerians.

As we said above the government accepted that the 301 multi-purpose local government areas be retained but then changed its mind on two occasions, as it had with state creation. By the end of May 1993 there were 589 local government areas in Nigeria, and more were promised. As Babangida said on May 26, 1993 just three months before he was due to hand over power "there are areas that definitely need the attention of the federal government as far as local government areas are concerned. He went on "if the various requests fit in we will create a few. It is not a wholesome exercise."[52] Doubling the number of local government areas and increasing by almost two-thirds, the number of states did serious damage to the financial and political viability of these crucial units of Nigerian federalism.[53]

As the Udoji Commission reported in 1974 when states and local governments were not receiving as much as presently from the Federation Account, only Lagos State had up to forty-four per cent of its total revenue internally generated. Some states generate no more than sixteen percent of their revenue internally. This creates unnecessary dependence on the central government and the tendency to install unitary government by the back door.

The government's acceptance of the recommendation of the Political Bureau for a two-party-system has been strongly criticised by many Nigerians for a variety of

---

[52] *National Concord*, Thursday May 27, 1993.
[53] On the issue of local government see Oyediran's "Local Government Development," in Larry Diamond *et al.*, *op. cit.*

reasons.[54] Here, however, our concern is with the degree to which the Babangida government honoured the letter and spirit of the Bureau recommendation which it accepted in its White Paper. The government heavily violated the democratic spirit of the Bureau recommendation. It is not possible to discuss this in detail here. Elsewhere Badejo documents the unfolding of this "drama".[55] The outline of government policy decisions and actions is given below.

With the lifting of the ban on partisan politics, Nigerians were allowed by government to form political associations. More than thirty of such associations emerged out of which thirteen applied to the National Electoral Commission (NEC) for registration at a cost of ₦50,000. They were thoroughly scrutinised by NEC in its report to the Armed Forces Ruling Council. A great part of the NEC report dealt with the nature and behaviour of the political associations during recruitment for membership. In summary, the report among other things claimed that old lines of cleavages – ethnic, religious, geopolitical and class resurfaced in the formation of the associations. This led to

---

[54] See, for example A.M. Jega, "The Viability of the Two-party System tin Nigeria" in I.E. Amdi and W. Hintary (eds), *Party system, Democracy and Political Stability in Nigeria*, Zaria, Ahmadu Bello University, Press, 1989; Anthony A. Akinola, "A Critique of Nigeria's Proposed Two-Party System," *Journal of Modern African Studies*, vol. 27, no. 1, March 1989, pp. 109-124; Anthony A. Akinola, "Manufacturing the Two-party system in Nigeria," *The Journal of Commonwealth and Comparative Studies*, Vol. XXVIII, No. 3, Nov. 1990, pp. 309-327. Peter Koehn, *op. cit.*, Proceedings of the Annual Conference of the Nigerian Political Science Association for 1987, 1988, 1989, and 1990; Oyeleye Oyediran and Adigun Agbaje, "Two Partyism and Democracy Transition in Nigerian," *The Journal of Modern African Studies*, vol. 29. no. 2, 1991, pp. 213 235.

[55] Babafemi A. Badejo, "Party Formation and Competition," in Larry Diamond *et al, op. cit.*

the decision of the AFRC not to recognise any of the associations but to create instead, two political parties that Nigerians were asked to join. These two political parties were named Social Democratic Party (SDP) and National Republican Convention (NRC). According to the AFRC the constitution of each of the two political parties was subject to the following guidelines:[56]

(a) the constitutions shall be identical;
(b) each shall emphasise representative democracy, republicanism, presidentialism, federalism, foreign policy goals, non-adoption of any religion as state religion, fundamental rights, basic freedoms and the two-party system;
(c) each shall provide modalities for accountability at an annual congress or convention;
(d)   each shall provide for the same:
    (i) number of officer, i.e. members of the executive committee;
    (ii) mode of financial accountability; and
    (iii) machinery for disciplining members;
    (iv) set of national values underwriting its programmes.

It was decided that the manifestos of the parties would "reflect an ideological spectrum, one a little to the left and the other, a little to the right, of the centre."[57] Finally, it was decided that the Federal Military Government would fund the two political parties. Party offices were built for each of the political parties at the local, state and federal levels. Party conventions were held as scheduled by government to elect officers for each political party at all levels of

---

[56] See *For Their Tomorrow we gave our today: Selected Speeches of IBB Volume 11*, Jersey C.L. U.K.: Satan Books Ltd., 1991, p. 21.
[57] Ibid., p. 22.

government. Before this, government appointed administrative secretaries for each party. NEC provided the membership cards and symbols. Members registered for the party of their choice at the local government level. The constitution and manifesto of each party were prepared by NEC and launched by General Babangida in November 1989.[58] As soon as the local, state and federal offices of each of the two parties were elected in 1990 there was continuous government interference in their functioning. In 1992, all elected officers of each of the two parties elected two years earlier were removed by government and replaced by bureaucrats and other government appointed officers. The latter were replaced in March 1993 by elected members of each political party. The control that NEC exerted on the political parties was unprecedented in the history of democratic political party formation and development in Nigeria or elsewhere. Not only did the parties get their government subvention through NEC, this super-election body, determined whether or not the campaigns mounted by the parties were conducted according to guidelines prepared by it, whether or not elections to the various offices of the parties were free and fair, as well as whether or not persons who wanted to run for offices were qualified.

---

[58] In an analysis of the manifestos of the political parties Isijola came to the conclusion that "There is no gainsaying that the evidence... indicate a close programmatic aping of the Republican Party (U.S.A.) by the NRC while the same is true of the similarity between the SDP and the Democratic Party (U.S.A.")"; Olu Isijola, "A Comparative Analysis of the Manifestos of Nigeria's Two Political Parties (SDP and NRC)" in Constitutionalism and National Development in Nigeria, Proceedings of the 17th Annual Conference of the Nigeria Political science Association held at the University of Jos, 21-23 November 1990, p. 394.

In many cases it did not have to give reasons for its decisions. Unaccountable for these decisions to anyone but the authoritarian military regime, NEC functioned in a manner that contradicted the spirit of democracy.

Though the Political Bureau report did not contain any specific recommendation on how the two recommended political parties were to be formed and developed, the members could not and did not anticipate that government would act like a "benevolent dictator" in setting up, naming and nurturing these two political parties, which many people began to refer to as government parastatals. The result of the military government actions nauseated many normally active politicians, to the extent that they refused to participate in the transition political process. Many waited for the return to civil rule and as in many other areas of public life in Nigeria, they waited for a new beginning, a new decision by the Nigerian people as to which way to go. The position was articulated loud and clear that the National Question, the form, structure and process of governance in Nigeria were yet to be answered. It could only be answered after the transition from military to civil rule was completed.[59] Strictly interpreted this meant that

---

[59] How else can we interpret the call by the Committee of Elder Statesmen which Babangida commended when the members paid him a visit during the last week of May 1993 - three months before Babangida left office. The Committee called for the creation of the office of Prime Minister because it ensures stability and power sharing and also insulates the presidency from the day to-day running of government, The Guardian Saturday May 29, 1993 pp. 1 and 2. One member of-this committee, Margaret Ekpo also belonged to the other which Babangida criticised strongly. This group was different from the Association for Democracy and Good Governance in Nigeria (ADGN) which Babangida abhorred. The latter group included civil and military leaders. They were Adebayo Adedeji, Datti Ahmed, David Iornem, Jacob Nwokolo, Margaret Ekpo,

the Babangida years with respect to the wishes of Nigerians as basis for political restructuring had been wasted years in the life of Nigeria. And this being so, the members of the

---

Bolanle Awe, Sarah Jibril, Mahmud Waziri, Olu Akinfosile, H.J.R. Dappa-Biriye, M.S. Hamza, Olusegun Obasanjo, Theophilus Danjuma,, Tunde Idiagbon, Jeo Garba, Muhamadu Buhari, Ebitu Ukiwe, and Alani Akinrinade. Others are Abubakar Rimi, Abubakar Mohammed, Ladi Jemi-Alade, S.O. Wey, Yaya Abubakar,, Lawan Dambazau, A.Y. Abbas, Olabiyi Durojaiye, Sola Saraki, Dele Fajemirokun, Teju Oyeleye, Rufai Mohammed and O. O. Onuoha.

This thirty-one member body was made up of two former military heads of state, two former military prime ministers (Chief of Staff) former executive secretary of the Economic Commission for Africa (ECA) former chairperson of National Women's Commission in Babangida's administration, two former chief of army, one former permanent representative to the United Nations, one former head of the civil service of the federation, one former civilian governor, one majority leader in the Senate., one former permanent secretary and one presidential contestant during the transition.

In the communiqué issued after its first meeting on 26th May 1993, the group resolved to work for:

a. eradication of decay within all institutions of government that threatens the very life of the nation;

b. the strengthening of fundamental federal structure of Government instead of replacing it with an absolutist government;

c. prevention of subversion of constitutional, administrative and social systems;

d. decentralisation of resource control and serious and determined action to reduce corruption which is normally encouraged by monopoly plus discretion minus transparency and accountability;

e. taking cognisance of foreign interest in our affairs and being mindful of our place within the global community".

Some members of this group claimed that they understood that all public institutions had totally collapsed. This probably arose from the four weeks strike of the staff of virtually all public institutions, local, state and federal during the last weeks of February and first weeks of March 1993.

Political Bureau also wasted not only their time, and energy in producing a report, they also wasted the resources of the nation by doing so.

Conclusion

There was nothing inherently wrong in what the military administration of General Babangida did by getting the Nigerian people to talk about their political future while the administration got on with the business of governing. Committees of enquiry, tribunals and such other bodies are set up by governments all the time and everywhere for a variety of reasons. Sometimes they are set up when governments do not want to take action on some issues. At other times, they are set up with the genuine motive of finding out what is wrong and what alternatives are open to governments in resolving the problems.[60] Those who criticise the Babangida administration for setting up the Political Bureau are, on this basis, unfair.

Some of the members of the Bureau, however, felt they were used. Many were invited to do one thing or the other for government throughout the life of the administration. Some profited from this "co-optation" and some were "settled". The fact that many of the members of the Bureau were political scientists made the Nigerian Political Science Association the envy of other academic associations. The NPSA was seen as the "governing association" replacing those formerly in power. This was a misconception as S.G. Tyoden argued:

---

[60] See Gerald Rhodes, *Committees of inquiry*, London, Royal Institute of Public Administration and George Allen and Unwin Ltd., 1975, pp. 11-12.

> There has indeed been an intimate romance
> between the regime (of Babangida) and some
> political scientists...but such relationship has been
> based on the self-recognition of such of our
> colleagues by the regime, on its own criteria of
> professional competence and relevance, which is a
> completely different thing from government's
> relationship with the association.[61]

In short individual members of the association might have been co-opted but not the association itself as a body.

Various questions were raised about the legacy of General Babangida's administration well before it approached its scheduled end. When such questions were raised by people who weigh their words carefully and were regarded by most Nigerians as patriots, then that administration's claim as an agent of positive social, economic and political change was called profoundly into question. Anthony Enahoro, who in March 1953 first moved the historic independence motion for Nigeria, said in March 1992 that "We cannot escape the fact that what we require in Nigeria after the transition (from Babangida's administration) is not continuity of its policies but discontinuation, not continuity of its programmes but a profound change of them."

He went on to ask what policies and programmes the Babangida administration wanted to hand over to its successor:

- Is it Structural Adjustment Programme and their economic policies which have proved so disastrous to the naira and to the common people of Nigeria?

---

[61] S.G. Tyoden, "Political Scientists and the Transition," *The Guardian*, Thursday, December 24, 1992, p. 13. Tyoden was then the Director of Research of the Nigerian Political Science Association.

- Is it their budgetary actions, which have outraged even former military leaders like General Olusegun Obasanjo and General Alani Akinrinade?
- Is it their fiscal management which has left the new civilian state governors with empty treasuries or their theatrical largesse which together have made our pleas for debt relief a sick joke around the financial capitals of the world?
- Is it their record of unemployment which has resulted in the closure of factories up and down the land and in mounting numbers of beggars in the streets?
- Is it their social policies which have produced a sharp decline in educational and moral standards not to mention an explosion in corruption and religious conflicts?
- Is it to the deification of wealth, with no obvious source of its sudden appearance?
- Is it in its attitude to 'open government' when you and I do not know who lifts Nigeria's oil which is the country's major source of income?
- Is it in the promotion of a free wheeling society where no questions are asked, so long as the end and the means coincide?[62]

Segun Osoba, former social historian at the Obafemi Awolowo University called Babangida the "one leader that has inflicted the greatest suffering on the Nigerian people."[63] General Danjuma observed that corruption in Nigeria became "so abrasive, so flagrant and pervasive that it is frightening."[64]

It is unfortunate that the Babangida administration ended its life under a very thick cloud of cynicism. This

---

[62] Quoted in *African Concord*, 13 April 1992, p. 27. Enahoro proudly and correctly stated that as one who staked his life's ambition for Nigeria and who particularly wants to be anything else at his age he felt ambitions have died" he lamented.

[63] Ibid., p. 28.

[64] Ibid., p. 34.

perhaps reached its culmination when Bolaji Akinyemi, former External Affairs Minister in Babangida's administration echoed Obasanjo's words that "a good morning from the government even when confirmed by the watch one is wearing, is still met by it cannot be morning - an attitude cultivated through betrayal of hope."[65] If there are any good things that the Babangida administration did to improve the quality of life of Nigerians, the prevailing mood of the people in the closing months of the regime's life overshadowed them. No civilian administration, it was widely accepted, could be worse than the military administration of General Babangida. Thus we agree with Onaolapo Soleye, a former federal minister of finance under the Buhari/Idiagbon administration, that many actions and designs of the Babangida administration were "a vehicle for subverting a democratic order in Nigeria."[66] It was only in this light that the government's Political Bureau report could be correctly seen. Once more, the late Chief Obafemi Awolowo was proved right when he said in 1986 when asked to contribute to the Political Bureau debate:

> I do fervently and will continue fervently to pray that I may be proved wrong. But something within me tells me loud and clear that we have embarked on a fruitless search. At the end of the day when we imagine the new order is here, we would be terribly disappointed.[67]

---

[65] *The Guardian*, Monday 17th May, 1993, P. 2.

[66] "Intervention by Dr. Ona Soleye," in Colloquium on the Transition Programme, hosted by the Nigerian Institute of Advanced Legal Studies, Lagos, Nigeria, Thursday March 18, 1993.

[67] Chief Awolowo's letter to the Executive Secretary of the Political Bureau, dated, March 24, 1986.

Malthouse Monographs on Africa

Editor: Dafe Otobo, DPhil (Oxford),
Professor, University of Lagos, Lagos, Nigeria

Advisory Editorial Board

Professor Adele Jinadu, Centre for Advanced Social Science, Port Harcourt, Nigeria.
Professor John Ohiorhenuan, UNDP, New York
Professor Eddie Webster, University of Witwatersrand, Johannesburg, South Africa
Gavin Williams, St Peter's College, University of Oxford, UK.

Malthouse Monographs on Africa

Malthouse Monographs on Africa are peer-reviewed works on Africa covering the six main areas of a) social sciences and development studies; b) history, law and international relations; c) environmental and agricultural studies; d) gender, refugee and conflict studies; e) strategic and defence studies; and f) labour and trades unions.

The monographs are intended to provide an arena for free contestation of ideas and as outlet for research and empirical studies on Africa in the areas indicated above. The monographs thus have no links with, nor funded by, any government or political party. Nor do the views expressed in them represent those of the editorial board.

Works for consideration may be of purely theoretical, or historical or applied in nature or policy-oriented. Such may be sent directly to the Editor as electronic files (dafeotobo2002@yahoo.co.uk) in Microsoft Word Rich Text format, or to the publishers (malthouse_press@yahoo.com}. Diskettes and hardcopies may also be sent to the publishers at the address on the imprint page. The aim is to publish accepted works within three months.

Malthouse Monographs on Africa
Numbers 1 – 9

Guest Series Editor: Dayo Oluyemi-Kusa,
*Director, External Conflict Prevention & Resolution,
Institute for Peace and Conflict Resolution, The
Presidency, Abuja, Nigeria*

Malthouse Press Limited
43 Onitana Street, Off Stadium Hotel Road,
Surulere, Lagos, Lagos State
E-mail: malthouse_press@yahoo.com
malthouse_lagos@yahoo.co.uk
Tel: +234 (01) -773 53 44; 0802 364 2402

All rights reserved. No part of this publication may be reproduced,
transmitted, transcribed, stored in a retrieval system or translated into any
language or computer language, in any form or by any means, electronic,
mechanical, magnetic, chemical, thermal, manual or otherwise, without the
prior consent in writing of Malthouse Press Limited, Lagos, Nigeria.

This book is sold subject to the condition that it shall not by way of trade,
or otherwise, be lent, re-sold, hired out, or otherwise circulated without the
publisher's prior consent in writing, in any form of binding or cover other than
in which it is published and without a similar condition, including this
condition, being imposed on the subsequent purchaser.

© Malthouse Monographs on Africa 2007
First Published 2007
ISBN 978 023 233 8

Distributors:
African Books Collective Ltd
Email: abc@africanbookscollective.com
Website: http://www.africanbookscollective.com

Guest Editor's comment

All the Monographs in this series attempt to explore and document events, policies and impact of the General Ibrahim Babangida-led military regime in Nigeria, covering the period 1985 to 1993. These contributions were originally for a book edited by me on that regime but other considerations, especially that of comprehensiveness of coverage of arguably the most momentous phase in Nigeria's post-Civil War socio-political development, led to the shelving of that idea. It was thought that a more useful scope or coverage might be achieved through a continuing development of Monographs on different facets of Nigerian society under this regime – a feat which may only be possible in a book so voluminous and whose cost might be such as to be out of the reach of the intended audience.

I should like to thank all the contributors who have waited this long to see their work in print, a fate that is unlikely to befall the contributors of the other titles currently in preparation. I am grateful to the publishers for including these titles in Malthouse Monographs for Africa family.

Dayo Oluyemi-Kusa

Politics of the annulment of June 12 presidential election in Nigeria

Professor Adekunle Amuwo
Executive Secretary
The African Association of Political Science (AAPS)
Pretoria, Republic of South Africa

No. 9

Contents

Introduction

Writing on ethnic dilemmas and the challenge of ethnicity to democracy in Africa, in the aftermath of the presidential election in Nigeria, Marina Ottaway (1995:22 24) notably observes that "the future of Zaire and Nigeria is in doubt." She elaborates:

> ...we can no longer assume that the political transformation of Africa will simply entail a change of regimes. The real danger is not the possibility of the break-up of some African countries into new states...but the collapse of an increasing number of states into utter chaos and mass slaughter.

While conceding that Nigeria and South Africa have shown a lot of realism in dealing with ethnicity in politics, she laments that:

> ...years of constitutional and political engineering since the Biafran civil war have been undermined by the two great constraints of Nigerian politics: the concentration of oil revenues in the hands of the federal government which precludes genuine decentralization and empowerment of state and local governments; and the constant intervention of the army in politics, which precludes democratization. In the end, Nigeria remains very far from both democracy and ethnic reconciliation.

The manipulation of electoral consultations as well as frenetic resistance to full-blown democratic openings is a major hallmark of ruler-ship by rent-seeking military and civilian political elite in much of Africa. The consequences have almost always been debilitating. But why resist democracy? Why annul critical elections? Crawford Young (1995:24) suggests an answer:

> Security forces hierarchies are...directly threatened by democratization as political opening almost invariably means an alteration of the cultural distribution of power". He adds that the responsibilities of these security forces "are very great in the failures of liberalization in Togo, Nigeria and Zaire, among others...

Aside the hierarchies of the security and armed forces, two other factors or variables were at work in the annulment of the June 12 presidential election and the subsequent robust attempts to politicise it by, amongst other modalities, ethnicising it. The first variable alluded to earlier, was a rentier state and the elites that benefit from it. In a fundamental sense, rent-seeking activities accentuate the predatory character of the post-colonial state in Africa, even though rents do not always have to be cast in a negative mould. Rents also tend to constrain many groups by diverting attention away from democratic goals to state patronage (Frischtak, 1994). Bratton (1992) has fleshed up this notion:

> Where political power has long been personalized and resources are still concentrated in the state, politics remains a matter of 'winner takes all'. Given the shortages of opportunity for upward mobility in the economy and in society, voters will continue to try to attach themselves to the coat-tails of those political patrons who seem closest to the fount of public largesse. Because it is too costly to dissociate oneself from the winners of competitive elections,

> opposition leaders routinely 'cross the floor'.
> All incentives point to aligning one's self with
> those ruling inside the state rather than with
> the opposition movements that are frozen
> 'outside' the patronage system.

More specifically, for Ake (1993), the character of politics in Nigeria is largely responsible for the foregoing phenomenon. He insists that:

> (Nigerian) politics is not a lawful competition to
> select those to manage our common concerns, but
> a fight to capture and privatise an enormous power
> resource. There is no public realm, strictly
> speaking, no state. There is only a contested
> terrain, where interest groups and communities go
> to fight for appropriation…

To be sure, a political praxis which leads each ethnic group to place itself strategically vis-à-vis its competitors is easily exacerbated in ethnically-segmented socio-economic formations. Interethnic rent-seeking politicking ensures, rather paradoxically, some form of ethnic balancing, however wretched. It also circumscribes the probability of ethnic conflagration.

It is an ever-present danger, though, for as long as the two major demands of most sub-ethnic groups in Nigeria, as elsewhere, are denied them, namely, political democracy and social justice. This is the point that both Ottaway and Bratton make. Ake (1991:34) disagrees, contending that there is nothing inherently conflictual about ethnic differences. For him, the latter "lead to strife only when they are politicised and it is the elite who politicise ethnicity in their quest for power and political support."

The immediate post-annulment period in Nigeria provides a rich data validating the Akean thesis.

The second variable at work is the character of the politics and management that sheer survival in a grossly disenabling socio-economic formation imposes on the mass majority, by virtue of accentuated pauperization.."Poverty and inequality," writes Weyland (1995:126), "pose more urgent problems for democratic stability." He adds that "without social guarantees, many of the poor are virtually forced into clientelist submission to the elite who provide minimal benefits in return for obedience." He also contends that the quality and survival of democracy are dependent, on the long run, on poverty-reduction and satisfaction of popular hopes for social improvements. One may add that not only many of the poor but, more significantly, many of the rich, cross-ethnically, with the tradition of living on and off the state, often lack the political capacity and moral muscle to assert autonomy when the state and its key agents and agencies make a detour into rampant illegalities - as the immediate post-June 12 1993 events copiously demonstrate.

If Nigeria has, till date, escaped the spectre of military-driven ethnic conflagration, it is largely due to the critical role of the country's civil society in its rich heterogeneity – which, by the way, is at once a source of strength and weakness. Some western governments, in particular Britain, the United States, many of the Scandinavian countries (even though they often are less vocal than the US and the UK) as well as some foreign-based CSOs and non-governmental organisations (NGOs), have also contributed to stiff opposition to civil hostilities. But, then, this is an ever-present option insofar as entrenched interests do not want to as much as entertain the idea that June 12 signalled the end of an *ancien regime* and the beginning of a new era, a new Nigeria.

This approach of state-civil society linkage has the potentiality of circumscribing the largely state-centric perspective one finds in much of the otherwise prolific outpourings of Africanist studies. In other words, following Mahmood Mamdani (1995:609), the state ought not to be "conceptualised (solely) as an exclusively institutional category", one whose "interest is seen as purely the interest of its managers." Rather, the question of state capacity (and incapacity) ought also to be seen as "simultaneously a condensation of social relations" which is intelligible only when "put in the context of a wider galaxy, struggles within civil society."[68]

There are many sides to the ensuing politics of the June 12 election. One of them, not necessarily the most popular, but arguably the most tangible in terms of values and principles in governing ethnically-segmented societies, is the struggle for recognition, which Hegel and Kojeve, a Russian émigré, identified as "the motive force of human history." As articulated by Plattner (1992:120), "the appeal of democracy does not lie simply in the attractions of prosperity and personal freedom but also has something to do with the desire to be recognized as the equal of any other citizen." Increasingly over time in developing economies, those fighting for recognition in electoral and democratic struggles often view democracy as an

---

[68] This perspective necessarily entails dialogue in concrete forms-whatever these are between the commanding heights of the state and leading organisational lights of civil society. Where dialogue is absent, the state experiences blockage in intellectual and legitimacy terms, thus directing its resultant frustration on key groups and individuals in civil society. An example of this phenomenon is the case of Uruguay. See Julio M. Sanguinetti, 1991:3-10.

"emancipatory project" (Ake, 1992: 36). In the language of Sartori (1995:102) "freeing the people" (liberalism) or "demo-protection" (meaning the protection of a people from tyranny) may be first sought for, in the hope that "empowering the people" (democracy) or "demo-power" (the implementation of popular rule) would be a natural follow-up. Heightened politicisation of power, property and poverty, in an extremely provocative and grotesque manner, arrested the people's perceived freedom via June12, thereby scuttling both popular rule and the people's empowerment.[69]

What follows is a somewhat detailed exposition and critical analysis of June 12 and its immediate aftermath until and a little beyond the *stepping aside* in a rather humiliating manner of General Ibrahim Babangida.

The June 12 1993 presidential election

It is not for nothing that the presidential election of June 12 1993 has been described not only as the fairest and freest in the country's electoral and political annals, but also as the most significant, in terms of its epochal value. The election broke down hitherto existing ethnic barriers and dealt a seeming death-blow to artificial cleavages.

---

[69] Chief M. K. O. Abiola, the unofficial winner of the election, made allusion to this complex phenomenon when he said that those who annulled the election must be those who had looted the national coffers and were therefore apprehensive of a probable Daniel come to judgement. See *African Concord* (Lagos) 6 June 1994, p. 17. Chief Abiola was the publisher of *African Concord*, Nigeria's first pan-African weekly. It was one of the many titles in the Concord publishing outfit.

Chief M.K.O. Abiola of the Social Democratic Party
(SDP) clearly overran Alhaji Bashir Tofa, his opponent
from the rival National Republican Convention (NRC).
Abiola's victory was as decisive as it was astounding. He
won hands down in nineteen of the then thirty states and
obtained the statutory one-third in nine others. He won in
nine of the sixteen northern states, three of the seven
eastern states and in all the seven western states; only in
Sokoto and Kebbi did he fail to obtain the mandatory one-
third of votes cast. What was more, Abiola defeated Tofa in
his home state of Kano. In Imo State, where hails Dr.
Sylvester Ugoh, Tofa's running mate, Abiola got 44.7% of
the votes cast.

The significance of this seeming revolutionary cultural
re-distribution of power has not been lost on many
perceptive scholars and observers. Claude Ake regards June
12 as "a historical breakthrough" in Nigeria. For him, it
was "the day the ordinary people of Nigeria rose against the
ethnic, religious and regional prejudices and the divisive
politics with which colonialism and the political class had
oppressed them for half a century." He adds that "in doing
this, they took a great step towards making Nigeria a truly
viable and democratic polity."[70] In the same vein, the
election has been seen as signifying the validity of the right
of any Nigerian to lead Nigeria. Thus, as a riposte against
Chief Ernest Shonekan - the man hand-picked by General
Babangida, some NRC and SDP bigwigs and remnants of
the Babangida vanguard as head of the Interim National
Government (ING) after Babangida's ouster - who said
Nigerians should forget June 12, Femi Otubanjo argues that
to do so would be "to alienate that right in perpetuity". He

---

[70] Claude Ake "Our Interim Future," *African Concord Special* October
1993, p. 63.

continues: "the cancellation, the ethnicisation of June 12 and the Interim National Government can only serve a purpose: keep the oligarchy permanently in power." And "unless we are willing to be slaves, we can't accept this and this is why we can't forget June 12."[71]

Until the abrupt stoppage of the release of election results on June 16, 1993 by the National Electoral Commission (NEC), many Nigerian voters were seemingly oblivious of high-level, behind-the-scene manoeuvres to halt the process. True, there was the Mrs. Justice Ikpeme Bassey order of June 10 asking NEC not to hold the election, but this move appeared ill-advised to most Nigerians to the extent that the regime had, through numerous decrees, put NEC above court injunctions. For instance, Decree 13 stipulated in Section 19(1) that:

> notwithstanding the provisions of the constitution of the Federal Republic of Nigeria, 1979, as amended or any other law, no interim or interlocutory order or ruling, judgement or decision

---

[71] Femi Otubanjo "Of Amnesia and Enslavement", ibid., p. 45. A week to the election, Lewis Obi, Editor-in-Chief of *African Concord*, had, in his column, asked a critical question, which was later to be a litmus test for the so-called emergent new political culture the Babangida junta claimed it was nurturing: "Can a southern Nigerian be president of Nigeria through the ballot box?" And the corollary: "If not, would the Federation of Nigeria be able to survive what would appear like a one-sided romance where the leadership is recruited only from a particular section?" Obi made a case for Abiola on the ground that he "is the only Southern politician to have built meaningful political bridges across Rivers Niger and Benue." And the political lesson: "Should Abiola fail, given his credentials and the enormous energy and resources he poured into it, it may lead to a feeling of hopelessness in the South and may render the Federation less secure as an entity." See Obi "Make or Break Possibly," *African Concord* 14 June 1993, p. 15.

made by any court or tribunal before or after the commencement of the decree, in respect of any intra-party dispute or any other matter before it, shall affect the date or time of the holding of the election or the performance by the Commission of any of its functions under this decree or any guidelines issued by it in pursuance of the election.

By the same token, Section 16 of the Transition to Civil Rule Decree 19 of 1989, as amended by Decree 52 of 1992, shielded NEC from litigation on electoral matters. There was, therefore, legally, no room for manoeuvre by the Association for Better Nigeria (ABN) or its national chairman, Chief Arthur Nzeribe, a multi-millionaire arms merchant who had declared himself bankrupt in the United Kingdom in the late 1970s. Such hatchet persons were outlawed by Section 11 of Decree 27 of 1989, as amended, which asked every citizen "to participate in and defend all democratic processes and practices." To complement this, Section 8 of Decree 19 of 1987 stipulated five years imprisonment without option of fine for any person that undermined the transition programme. It was, therefore, surprising that Nzeribe and the ABN were left free to pursue their open agenda of derailing the transition programme. The government's standard response to rumbles in civil society was that it was their inalienable right to do so. Yet, the same right was not extended to critics of the programme.

Nzeribe and his ABN carried out their activities in all quietude apparently because General Babangida was aware the organisation was working for him and he fully supported it. A court order to the organisation to stop its 'national rally' in Abuja on Election Day was ignored. The plan was to present to Shonekan, then head of the

Transitional Council, alleged 20 million signatures of Nigerians calling on Babangida to stay on, which was another way of saying that the election itself should be stopped. The bizarre thing was that the ABN got a police permit for the rally.

The big plot on the eve of June 12, according to Abimbola Davis, national director of organisation of ABN who later confessed on television was "Abiola must not be the next president and Babangida must remain president after August 27 (1993)."[72] Babangida would become a civilian president and Nzeribe, his prime minister.[73] The ABN was determined to achieve its objective of thwarting the election. The junta found it all too convenient to support the organisation and use it as a smokescreen. The point is that after so many detours in the transition programme as well as postponement of handing over date on three occasions, the regime found it well-nigh difficult to shift disengagement date again. The domestic and international publics were already very sceptical, if not altogether cynical.

The Ikpeme order to stop the June 12 election was the climax of activities by ABN that were often less than successful. For one, the plan was to disrupt the election and

---

[72] See S. Ohumhense "The Big Plot against Democracy," *TELL* (Lagos) August 2, 1993, p. 16.

[73] This semi-presidential system of government *a la francaise* was recommended on the eve of the election by a Committee of Elders, organised by the former radical journalist with Chief Awolowo's *Nigerian Tribune* (lbadan), Tola Adeniyi. The members included another former 'socialist', Sam Ikoku and Margaret Ekpo, a well-known female nationalist of the pre-independence period. Curiously, the Committee was received in audience, with much media blitz, by General Babangida, even though he did not constitute the team *ab initio*.

this was to begin from Kano. It was in the same city that on June 6, same year, a group - Committee for National Unity - addressed a press conference on the need to give Babangida four more years in office. Curiously, the *alibi* canvassed was that Nigeria's first military president had failed to fulfil his promises. For another, on June 9, in another northern town - Kaduna - opponents of return to civil rule, apparently sponsored by the ABN, went round the town in a convoy denouncing the election and eulogizing military dictatorship. One inscription read "IBB (Ibrahim B. Babangida): We need you for another four years." Another inscription passed the unwholesome verdict: "Civil Rule is Cruel."[74]

As we will show later, that Nzeribe, a scion of the SDP not only in the Eastern states, but also nationally, was not sanctioned, was because Baba Gana Kingibe, the foundation chairperson of the party, was working for both the presidency and the ABN. Indeed, Nzeribe had, like (the now late) retired General Shehu Yar'Adua, financed Kingibe's chairmanship bid of the SDP in 1989. The two of them invested a lot of money in the People's Front (PF), which, until the dissolution of the two parties in November 1993 by the Abacha junta, was the most dominant tendency in the SDP. The struggle to control the SDP was intense between Nzeribe and Yar'Adua The former was particularly desperate apparently because he had promised Babangida that he would place the party at his disposal. The partnership between the two politicians was, not

---

[74] ABN's secretary-general in Katsina State, Bily Saulawa, who also resigned in the aftermath of the annulment, lamented in a press statement that leaders of the group had played all sorts of tricks on members with a view to derailing the transition programme. He claimed he did not know this until a few days to June 12.

unexpectedly, an uneasy one. They finally fell apart on account of personal presidential ambitions. Soon after, Nzeribe transformed his power machine into the ABN. Given his solid security service background - being one of the very few spies to be trained by the Nigerian government - Kingibe was perceived as a safer and more malleable candidate than Abiola.[75]

The Annulment

Whilst both national and intentional observers were agreed that the June 12 presidential election was the best ever conducted in the country,[76] there were some minor dissensions arising from it. As soon as it appeared it was heading for defeat, the NRC announced that it may contest

---

[75] This does not in any way suggest that had Kingibe won the Jos SDP presidential primaries and, eventually, the presidential election, the election would not have been annulled all the same. It can also be argued that the junta lost interest in the election once its preferred candidate was not in the race. It was national and extra-national outcry that saved the election. The major point, however, is that having survived no fewer than eleven major crisis, including two anti-SAP riots engineered by university students in 1988 and 1989 and the devastating Orkar coup in 1990, Babangida may have seen the annulment as merely one more crisis that he would roughshod over. His notion of politics was essentially zero-sum: whilst civil society loses everything, he and his politico-military cabal wins everything (Amuwo, 1995).

[76] They also underlined its significance. I have already made reference to the views of some nationals. The British newspapers were particularly instructive in this respect. With a rider 'voters pick man with rags-to-riches story as their president,' *The Independent* (15-6-93) announces that 'populist Yoruba chief looks set to lead Nigeria." More poignantly, perhaps, is the headline of *The Guardian*, "Nigeria's poll ends north's dominance.'

the election result on two legal grounds. One, that neither Tofa nor Ugoh was accredited to vote; the one because he had an old voter's card; the other because he apparently did not register - he only had what he said was a photocopy of his card. Two, that Abiola broke the ban on the use of campaign materials on Election Day. Abiola had voted donning a traditional *agbada* dress with the white horse, the SDP party symbol, emblazoned on the front. The NRC was also willing to make a case for annulment out of the alleged protests by minority Ogoni freedom fighters which led to the cancellation of the polls in the area after electoral officers and their equipment had been carted away in many local government areas.

Few gave much credit to these essentially legal and technical matters. At any rate, the overall results were already known by virtually everybody, even though NEC had announced results for only fourteen of the thirty states. When it appeared the NEC Chairman, Professor Humphrey Nwosu, was acting too independently and could announce the country's president-elect without any reference to the presidency, the Attorney-General, Clement Akpamgbo, broke protocols to serve the Abuja Chief Judge's injunction against further announcement on Nwosu. The latter's offer to resign was rejected. From then on, it was not NEC, but the presidency, meaning *stricto sensu,* Babangida and ABN, that were in charge, drawing the contours and determining the trajectory of the unfolding drama, in the process raising the political temperature to an all-time high.

The first act of the Babangida-ABN tandem was to cause NEC to suspend the election results. A terse statement emanated from NEC saying that:

> ...in the light of the current developments, the Commission has, in deference to the court

injunction and other actions pending in court,
decided to stay action on all matters pertaining to
the presidential election until further notice.

The statement signed by Nwosu, carried two dates,
June 12 and 16, suggesting that the annulment was pre-
meditated. To all appearances, the Babangida regime's plan
was to stalemate the election, with some key NRC-
controlled states (Sokoto, Kebbi, Bauchi, Niger and Rivers)
being slated to be used for that purpose.

The grand strategy was to rig the election in these
states and use them to counterbalance whatever massive
votes Abiola was expected to receive from the country's
western flank-Oyo, Osun, Ogun, Ondo, Lagos and Kwara.
In other words, a regime that, for eight long years, had
claimed its transition programme was intended to effect a
clean break with the geopolitical and ethnic arithmeticking
of the past was, itself, thinking and working largely in the
context of the same old, discredited parameters. According
to a source,

> ...the plot failed to reckon with the Nwosu
> factor...and this led to arrest of several NEC
> electoral officials in Sokoto, Kebbi, and Rivers
> States. The schemers' nightmare had become a
> reality and faced with the *fait accompli* of Abiola's
> resounding victory, the government pulled out the
> Justice Saleh joker...Nwosu was badly burnt in the
> process...he was literally compelled to sign the
> suspension order.[77]

---

[77] See Ike Okonta "Challenging the Voice of God," *The News* (Lagos)
28 June, 1993, p. 20.

It was this old wine-in-new bottle approach to socio-political engineering - meaning that Nigerians' political behaviour would remain ethnic-driven, notwithstanding a long-winding and costly transition programme - that partly informed the regime's decision to do little or nothing to stop Abiola until after the historic election. Shortly before the election, the junta flew a kite *a propos* of its intention to further prolong the transition programme. There was a statement that it would keep to the disengagement date of August 27, 1993 - the anniversary date of Babangida's 1985 coup which had, by then, virtually replaced October 1st, the Independence Day, in the hierarchy of dates - but, then, there was a caveat. The regime thought "it would be a business ended in error if the objectives of the transition programme were crashed at the presidential stage on altar of time constraint." There was also a press report - ostensibly leaked by the presidency - that Abiola and Tofa would have to scale new screening and clearance hurdles, barely three weeks to the election. Moreover, the junta could have seized upon the protest of some the National Electoral Commission's commissioners, formally lodged to the presidency, on alleged irregularities during the presidential primaries of the two parties in March 1993. Two irregularities in particular came up for mention. The first centred on alleged massive use of money by the presidential aspirants. The implicit suggestion was that neither Abiola nor Tofa won their parties' tickets on merit. Indeed, the commissioners' report was damaging. It said that compared to the botched primaries of August and September 1992, the reckless use of money to bribe and corrupt delegates was a sickening moral bogey.[78] The junta

---

[78] Shetima Ali Monguno, a former petroleum minister and veteran politician who was in the NRC, testified to this phenomenon. For

seemingly laid this matter to rest, only to revisit it and put it to a disingenuous use as an *ex-post facto* rationalisation for the annulment.

The second alleged irregularity related to the technical illegality the national conventions of the two parties committed by allowing Alhaji Abubakar Atiku and Chief Joe Nwodo, respectively of SDP and NRC, to withdraw in the second stanza of the elections. The commissioners pointed to the law that says that the first three aspirants would go on to the second round of the election.[79] As I mentioned earlier, the junta was under intense national and intentional pressure to conclude the transition. Voters (and observers alike) had become election-fatigued. This was, apparently, what saved the day.

The second act of the tandem in question, the more reprehensible one, was the annulment, pure and simple, of the presidential election. A presidential election (basic constitutional and transitional provisions) repeal decree no. 39 of 1993 enacted on June 22 1993 annulled the election. The annulment was justified on so many grounds, the most overarching being the nebulous and umbrella-like national interest. According to Babangida, "(my) administration

---

him, money politics was it: "money exchanged hands physically, openly at the Conventions to the full knowledge of the authorities and yet we went on...I thought Babangida should have stopped the elections, rather than allowing it and later on nullifying it." ("Option A4 was a big joke, says Monguno" *The Guardian* on Sunday, April 7, 1996, p. A5 and A6.

[79] The NEC commissioners who protested were not unanimous on this point. Some of them believed, like many politicians and voters, that the conventions were not only a supreme testimony of the readiness of the much-maligned 'political class' to take over power, but also constituted the triumph of option A4 (used in the election of aspirants from ward, local and state levels) and the silencing, at long last, of the numerous critics of the transition programme.

took the painful decision in good faith and in the interest of stability and security of the nation as well as for the enhancement of democracy in Nigeria." The regime cited probable judicial anarchy; the monetisation of the election; conflict between the personal interests of the presumed president-elect and national interest; low voter turn-out and, much later, the non-acceptability of Abiola's personality and candidacy to the armed forces.

According to a view, the first rationalisation for annulment – "to protect our legal system from being ridiculed and politicised" - qualifies as "the most original, if not the most cynical, excuse for cheating voters of their rights."[80] Much the same could be said about the other justificatory remarks for the annulment. Concerning the reckless use of money in the election, the regime had no moral right whatsoever to complain. Whilst repeatedly reiterating its determination to cultivate a class of new breed politicians, untainted by the moneyed politics of the preceding republics, the junta encouraged moneyed politics in practice. Not only did it create the two official parties and funded them somewhat lavishly, with scant regard for accountability,, it also looked the other way when the NRC and SDP required its presidential aspirants in August and September 1992 to obtain forms respectively with ₦500,000 and ₦400,000. In the process, many a worthy candidate lacking financial muscle was disallowed. Indeed, in a fundamental sense, the presidency was a veritable war of multi-millionaires; only few of the men - and women - who volunteered to serve their people at the apex were, in monetary and material terms, Lilliputians.

In any event, the accusation of exchange of money for massive voters remained unproved. Contemporary global

---

[80] See "Nigerian Follies" in *The Times* (London) 24 June, 1993.

literature on elections tends to suggest that many voters vote for personalities and not for ideas. And if and when rich presidential candidates merely benefit from their influence and popularity, money may erroneously be used to explain the success. Geremek (1992:11) says that "politics is focusing increasingly on the personalities of candidates rather than on parties and their programmes." Part of an on-the-ground assessment of the Abiola victory reads like this: "in most parts of the country, the results were at once a call for change, a repudiation of some of the incumbent governors and a vote for Abiola's person."[81]

I am not suggesting, for all of the foregoing, that Abiola and the SDP did not spend a lot of money on the elections. Of course, they did. So also did the NRC. The point, however, is that unlike what the Babangida's annulment alibi suggests, other factors worked in favour of Abiola. In Akwa Ibom and Cross Rivers states, it was reported that many youths openly rejected monetary inducements from NRC agents. Even where they accepted such offers, they still voted for the SDP. In Akwa Ibom, an NRC-controlled state, it has been suggested that only huge amounts of money from the government house helped the NRC to obtain the respectable score (48.14%) of the votes as against 51.86% for the SDP. NRC faithfuls alienated by the poor-performance of Governor Akpan Isemin could not have been mobilised otherwise.[82] Furthermore, the junta only wanted to take a revenge on Abiola and his entourage for the defeat inflicted on Kingibe at the primaries. I have already mentioned that Kingibe was sponsored by the presidency and the ABN. For the Jos convention, he got

---

[81] See Fred Ohwahwa: It's a new day well, almost," *The African Guardian* (Lagos) June 28, 1993, p.21.

[82] Ohwahwa, p. 19.

₦150 million from the presidency, while Nzeribe obtained ₦124 million from the same source. Since Abiola had already being perceived as the candidate to beat, the singular injunction was to fight him to a standstill.[83]

On the third alibi- conflict between personal and national interest- the junta was concerned to demonstrate that a president to whom his country was indebted could hardly protect national interest. But it is instructive to note that whereas both Abiola and Tofa were initially so characterised and implicated, the latter's name simply disappeared when supposed relevant documents were leaked to the press about the extent of federal government's indebtedness to Abiola. The documents subtly sought to play up Abiola as too much entrenched in the Nigerian system to be the messiah the civil society seemingly made of him. But they fell flat on their faces, and ended up indicting more the junta- and some governments before it- that had awarded the contracts and had paid huge sums of money even for jobs said to have been unsatisfactorily done. The Babangida regime, on this last point, paid US$684 million to Abiola's companies as well as to companies in which he had interests. These were payments previous governments had refused to make. Between 1985 and 1990, the junta awarded ten contracts to the said companies. Four of them, concerning supply of equipments and spare parts to NITEL, cost US$4.5 million. On the whole, "for these contracts and loan repayments made to ITT within that period, the federal government paid out US$196,933,113.34. By the same token, between 1960 and 1993, the junta claimed that ITT (Nigeria) and Radio Communications of Nigeria, RCN (one of Abiola's companies), were awarded contracts worth ₦43.7

---

[83] Confidential source

billion."[84] The junta was silent on whether or not all the contracts had been completed and all the money had been paid.

The untold story in the foregoing is that there was a pact amongst three friends, Babangida, Abiola and Abacha, to rule Nigeria in succession. Once Babangida seized power in 1985, he put at the disposal of his two friends wide-ranging facilities to make a lot of easy money. As successively General Officer Commanding (GOC), the First Mechanised Division of the Nigerian Army in Ibadan; Chief of Army Staff and Defence Minister, General Abacha had opportunities for self-enrichment. Even allocations statutorily earmarked for the army welfare, emoluments, etc., were misappropriated by Abacha without Babangida being able to call him to order. It was this *laissez-faire* attitude of Babangida to Abacha that led to the latter being appointed to the Interim National Government (ING) as Defence Secretary ostensibly to protect and defend interests of the political wing of the military. He would later use the ambiguous clause in the ING decree- that in the event of the incapacitation of the head of that government, the most senior secretary, should take over to oust Shonekan in a bloodless, palace coup on November 17, 1993.

The argument of low voter turn-out also sounds hollow. About 30 per cent of registered voters - some 14 million people - voted in the June 12 election. This is a universal trend. Dahl (1992:47) argues that "only a

---

[84] See Nats Agbo "Why Abiola was blocked" in *Newswatch* July 12, 1993 p. I0- I1. Few believed the authenticity of these claims, including the allegations that the SDP and Abiola had voted huge sums of money to bribe NEC officials. A retired general was quoted as saying that "these documents could be the beginning of a process of misinformation". Subsequent events proved him right. In Agbo, p. 11

minority of citizens is deeply interested in politics. Except for voting even fewer actively engage in politics." Sartori (1995:104) believes that "...the importance of voting tends to be exaggerated by authors who lack historical perspective." For an equally important transitional election (presidential) in Zambia in 1991, the voter turn-out was only 45 per cent and it was not cancelled on that ground (Bratton, 1992: 93).

More specifically, in comparative Nigerian terms, the voter turn-out was not altogether a poor one. In a one-page advert entitled *June 12: The Real Issues*, a group of well-known Nigerian politicians cutting across often exaggerated ethnic and cultural cleavages, punctured the poor voting argument. The politicians were Sam Mbakwe, Lateef Jakande, Eric Aso, Balarabe Musa, Ango Abdullahi and Yohana Madaki. They notably wrote that the turn-out was "35 per cent compared with between 31 and 33 per cent recorded in all elections in 1979 or compared with 29 per cent recorded during the 1991 governorship election of the (Babangida) transition programme." The politicians added, perhaps for effect, that "President Bill Clinton of the US got elected in an election that recorded about 37% voters' turn-out."[85]

The ABN apparently engineered the propaganda of low voter turn-out only to be appropriated by the government-owned daily, *New Nigerian*. The basic contention was that if only 12 million out of 40 million registered voters cast their votes on June 12, the result could not be representative of the people's will. For the tabloid, "no genuine leadership and credible democratic process can be installed or nurtured under such disastrously low voters' turn-out." To all appearances, this editorial was

---

[85] In *African Concord* (Special), October 1993, p.2

planted by the junta with full knowledge of Tofa. Walter Ofonagoro, latter's campaign director of publicity, had boasted that the election results (then coming out in trickles) would not stand. He told newsmen "if you doubt me, you should read the *New Nigerian* tomorrow."[86]

On the alleged refusal of officers and men of the armed forces of Nigeria to accept Abiola as their President and Commander-in-Chief, shreds of evidence were conspicuous by their absence. The so-called *imminent convulsion theory* of Augustus Aikhomu, Babangida's deputy, to the effect that Abiola was not popular in the barracks was not borne out on the ground. Whereas an inner caucus of senior military officers loyal to Babangida worked out plans for another extension of military rule a week to the election, a legion of equally senior officers undoubtedly favoured June 12. Their argument was that it not only crowned eight years of transition, a resultant Abiola government would halt the continued disintegration of the military and the undermining of professionalism in its ranks-and-file. There is a general agreement amongst the hierarchy of the military and students of civil-military relations in that the Nigerian military had metamorphosed from a partially progressive armed forces that enlisted radicals like Major Kaduna Nzeogwu and his co-coupists of January 15, 1966 to an army of "anything goes" to borrow the unhappy phraseology of Lt. General Salihu Ibrahim, a retired Chief of Army Staff. In all military barracks nation-wide, over 95 per cent of officers and men and their families voted for Abiola. By the annulment, not only the hope of a new

---

[86] Cf. Editorial "Our Nation, Our Destiny," June 16, 1993

Nigerian nation, but that of rebuilding the army faded away.[87]

Somehow, this non-acceptability argument eventually became an exercise in disingenuity. In an editorial entitled "Leave us alone", a direct reference to the negative reactions of the West, in particular the UK and the US, to the annulment. *The Citizen,* a rabidly pro-government weekly, argued that since a fresh election before the 27 August 1993 handover date looked "like a tall order" and since "any outcome of an election different from that of June 12 may be unacceptable to those who won it", it submitted that "the logical thing to do is to restore the June 12 election." The weekly's editorialists said "the authorities are unlikely to do that." Consequently, the onus was said to be on the political class, which "must realise they now have a historic responsibility to bring forth a southern candidate who is acceptable to all sections of the country and harbours no malice against any."[88]

If the military *qua* Nigerian military could not be held responsible for the annulment, there is hardly any doubt that an inner ruling caucus of military hawks and the personal ambitions of Babangida to rule Nigeria for as long as possible were responsible. It was this segment of the

---

[87] See Editorial of *The Guardian* (Lagos) "An Evasion of Reality" in *African Concord,* Ibid. p.26: "What the nation needs to face now is the urgent task of regeneration and rebuilding. Such a task belongs to a government with a popular mandate. Fortunately, such a government was elected on 12 June. The moment has produced its men; the emergency has furnished its resolution."

[88] Umaru Shinkafi, a former Nigerian Security Organisation (NSO) boss and an ex- presidential aspirant under the NRC has a different view, however. For him, "if ever there is a southerner than can be considered as nationally acceptable, it is Chief Abiola." For both views, see *The Citizen* (Kaduna) June 28, 1993, pp. 6-7, 12-13.

junta that continually led the military to violate its
commission oath to protect the territorial integrity of the
country as well as aid civil power to govern well and
maintain law and order. It was this group the then Sultan of
Sokoto, Alhaji Ibrahim Dasuki, was referring to when he
said that "we feel seriously unhappy on the charge that the
whole problem (of annulment) is created because a clique
in the army is opposed to Abiola being the president of
Nigeria."[89]

The point has to be made that whilst Abiola cut the
image of a civilian saviour in the eyes of the other ranks in
the military, he was seen as a villain by the army's high
command. The major grouse against him seems to be that
he had allegedly consistently put his immense wealth to
poor use, which consisted of sponsoring coups and showing
open disrespect to military chieftains.[90] Many of them
believed, rightly or wrongly, that Abiola would be
uncontrollable as the country's executive president. The

---

[89] In "The Military's Holding the Nation Hostage," *African Concord* 12
July, 1993, p.9. Sometimes, ethno-regional response overlaps with the
military factor. Halilu Akilu, a leading light of the caucus and
Babangida's security chief was quoted as saying soon after the
annulment: "Abiola would be president over my dead body" in ibid.

[90] In 1987, Abiola had a rough brush with some air force officers. He
and one of his sons were detained. On his release, the military was
unhappy that he set much store by the appellation of 'mad dogs'
which was how a senior air force officer had described military boys
to Abiola in private. His newspaper, *National Concord*, carried a
series of articles on what later became known as the 'mad dog
syndrome'. The following year, Abiola, irked that military governors
in the western states of Oyo, Ogun and Ondo kept away from his
installation as the *Aare Onakakanfo* (Supreme Military
Generalissimo) of Yorubaland by the Alafin of Oyo, referred to the
governors, in disdain, as 'Eaglet Governors' (that is under-aged;
Eaglet is the name of the country's under-17 soccer team)

military chieftains were more afraid of the Abiola entourage in which radicals like Gani Fawehinmi, the well-known activist Lagos lawyer and Balarabe Musa, impeached Second Republic Governor of Kaduna State, were very visible. This explains why few or none of them believed one of Abiola's promises during his electioneering campaign not to probe the military. Abiola had said that to do this would amount to "running forward and looking back", and running the risk of falling flat on one's face.[91] In the midst of the foregoing, Babangida was busy pursuing his own private agenda: as soon as he knew that Abiola had won, he phoned him offering him Prime Minister-ship for two years. Abiola rejected the offer.[92]

Kabiru Yusuf was therefore right to have counselled Abiola to look elsewhere, outside the North for explanation for the annulment. Abiola had, in some unguarded utterances, either said clearly or insinuated that the North did not want him, a southerner, a Yoruba multi-millionaire businessman, to occupy the highest political office in the land. Yusuf notably wrote:

> ...if Chief Abiola does not have an easy ride to the presidency, as many before him did not, it should now be clearer where the problem lies. It is the present military government (Babangida's), which has, for more than ten years, subverted the will of the Nigerian people.

After comparing the many games Babangida had played with the political class with the annulment, Yusuf concluded her thoughtful essay thus: "the difference this time is that an election has been held; the people have

---

[91] *African Concord* 21 June, 1993, p.26
[92] *Newswatch* July 12, 1993, p. 14.

spoken; their leaders should stand together to face the one remaining obstacle to full democracy."[93] But did they?

Ethnicisation of the annulment

We have already remarked that Babangida's overall strategy to perpetuate himself in power was double-pronged: destroy the old political class and create a new one totally loyal to him. The strategy had met with huge success until the annulment became the general's political *nunc dimitis*. Given the general Nigerian politicians' consummate opportunism, greed and unprincipled sentiments, Babangida had almost a field day to divide them in order to better dominate and rule them. For one, virtually every politician who has some prominence or visibility in his local government area or state of origin wants to have a go at the presidency. By January, 1993 when NEC began screening for the presidential election, there were no fewer than 271 presidential aspirants. For another, soon after a new presidential election was slated for August 1993 after the annulment, some of the twenty-three aspirants banned in 1992 but un-banned as part of the politics of the June 12 annulment did collect forms. Notable among them were Yar'Adua and Chief Emmanuel Iwuayanwu, the multi-millionaire publisher of *The Champion* newspapers. Joseph Wayas, Second Republic Senate President who was also Cross River state's candidate to the NRC presidential primaries in March 1993, was also involved.

---

[93] Kabiru Yusuf, "The People's Agenda," *The Citizen*, 28 June, 1993, p. 29

Dr. Chukwuemeka Ezeife, Third Republic governor of SDP-controlled Anambra state was therefore right in his observation that "most Nigerian politicians have no address when it comes to ideology. Most of them will have their address as 'where money is available' or which group is likely to win power to plunder the economy."[94] Yet, before and immediately after the election and its annulment, sheer political opportunism as well as geo-ethnic cleavages were hardly visible. All - or almost - rallied around Abiola and his mandate, generally regarded as a historic first-time victory for the progressive tendency in Nigerian politics. Abiola's support was then at once trans-ethnic, cross-cultural and supra-national.

Just before the election, a group of Nigerians cutting across ethnic groups organised victory rallies' for Abiola, prompting the chief sponsor to say that it was the first tune Nigerians abroad would assemble under one umbrella, irrespective of their ethnic background, to show their support for a candidate in a pan-Nigerian election.[95] Saleh Michika, Adamawa state governor, known for both bad and good humour, appealed to Nigerians

> ...whether they are NRC or SDP, whether they are from the north or south, to support Bashorun Abiola as the next President, because he is the best material among all other presidential aspirants and the most suitable to rule Nigeria today.[96]

---

[94] *The News* (Lagos) March 20, 1995, p. 14

[95] See "Victory Rallies for MKO Abiola," *African Concord*, 7 June, 1993, p.32

[96] See O. Adeniyi "Bashorun M. K. O Abiola ...Citizen of the World," in ibid., pp. 16-17. Michika would say later that no northerner should vote for a southerner in the presidential election. *African Concord*, 21 June 1993, p. 9

Soon after the annulment, the negative reaction and outpouring was nearly unanimous amongst politicians and other Nigerians alike. False notes were very few. Kingibe captured the mood of the political class when he observed that "...no man ever in the history of election in this country... will have the kind of mandate that Chief Abiola received on 12 June."[97] Haruna Izah believed that

> the lesson for the north as a whole be it the far north or the middle-belt is that its salvation lies not with a nostalgia for its once unquestioned political dominance, but a realignment with progressive ideals, nation-wide, regardless of who leads this crusade.[98]

Abubakar Rimi, who would later serve as Abacha's first communications minister, warned that "no attempt should be made by anyone, covertly or overtly, directly or indirectly, to tamper with the verdict of the people. Nobody should be allowed to put the nation on fire." [99] Even in Sokoto state where Abiola had his least support - 21.8% - the mood among SDP supporters was despondent. A leading party man there, Arzika Tanbuwal, declared that "we do not believe that there can be a better election than the one held on 12 June 1993." After its meeting on September 21 1993 at Damaturu, the North-East zone of the SDP (comprising Adamawa, Bauchi, Borno, Taraba and Yobe states) upheld the sanctity of the party's resounding victory on 12 June.[100] It dissociated itself not only from the

---

[97] Kingibe "Abiola must be President," in *African Concord Special*, p. 38

[98] H. Izah "This Cancer of Complicity," *Special*, pp. 30-31

[99] In *African Concord* 28 June, 1993, p. 17.

[100] See "Our Stand: North-East Zone of SDP" in *Special*, p. 49.

party chairman, Chief Tony Anenih's vacillations on the result, but also from the 'so-called Northern Elders Consultative Forum' and from their statements "which we consider parochial and dangerous to the peace, unity and stability of this country."[101] The Elders had earlier called for the dissolution of the political parties.

There were other reactions. Ojo Maduekwe, former special adviser to Kingibe, averred that:

> keeping to the 12 June mandate and swearing in Bashorun MKO Abiola as President of the Federal Republic on 27 August 1993 is not only the civilised thing to do, it is also the only feasible approach in the direction of national stability and international legitimacy.[102]

When a new election was mooted by Babangida, Mbakwe Second Republic governor of Imo state retorted:

> we look forward to 27 August when he (Abiola) will be sworn in as the elected president of Nigeria. The people of the East are totally opposed to another round of election.[103]

Alex Ekwueme, vice-president in the Second Republic, who would later become the rallying figure for an anti-

---

[101] This was one of the threats issued by Babangida to the SDP which, for a while, stood its ground on the June 12 election. The NRC had buckled under from day one. This was also an ABN agenda, failing which it wanted to become a third party, Association for Better Democratic Nigeria (ABDN). Abacha would later implement this policy-thrust, dissolving not only the parties, but also all other democratic structures.

[102] Ojo Maduekwe "A Nation on the Brink," in *Special,* p. 21.

[103] *African Concord*, 12 July 1993 p. 25.

military, and ostensibly progressive, political agenda at the National Constitutional Conference (NCC) of the Abacha junta, saw the annulment as "an executory pre-emptive coup against a government in anticipation." He was, however, clear in his mind that "any attempted resolution of Nigeria's present political problems which fails to take into account the 12 June elections will do irreparable damage to Nigeria's unity and stability."[104]

In what he regarded as politicians last chance to unseat soldier-rulers, Ebenezer Babatope, a scion of Awolowo's Unity Party of Nigeria (UPN) in the Second Republic who would later serve as Abacha's first transport and aviation minister, counselled his colleagues thus:

> ...leaders of the SDP and NRC must shun compromise, reject opportunism and leave the Nigerian soldiers to give us the wonder solutions that they believe will solve the political problems of Nigeria once and for all time.

He added: "the Nigerian people have spoken. They have given their mandate to MKO Abiola. On that, we must never waver."[105] Jakande, Abacha's first Works and Housing minister and arguably the *primus inter pares* in the Executive Council, agreed with him: "We have had an election on 12 June, and the people have elected Abiola. That is where the country stands."[106] In one of his many open letters to Babangida after the annulment, the head of the Anglican Church Communion in Nigeria, the Right

---

[104] A. Ekwueme "Where do we go from here?" in *Special* p. 60-61.
[105] E. Babatope "Their Final Test," in ibid., p. 23.
[106] *African Concord*, 12 July 1993, p. 25.

Reverend Abiodun Adetiloye, spoke of the need to uphold the election, but not without a tinge of spiritual foreboding:

> Nigeria may not come out of this crisis as one entity and God and history will forget whatever good you may have done and remember you as a military dictator who, for one reason or the other, took over power in a palace coup d'etat in August 1985. And because he was holding the butt of the gun, hardened his heart, destroyed the largest black country with his iron fist and led it into complete disintegration.[107]

Once Babangida saw that the annulment was widely rejected, he resorted to playing his old game of divide-and-rule, which consists of such elements as ethnicity, religion, money, threat, intimidation and subterfuge. The overall strategy was to meet, separately, with various groups, including politicians and executives of the two political parties to rationalise the annulment. Omnibus security reports were used to discredit both Tofa and Abiola, even though only the ones allegedly relating to the latter were made public. This instrument was exploited to convince almost all the governors against the Abiola mandate. Babangida did more a propos of the latter: he read a riot act

---

[107] *African Concord*, 26 July 1993, p. 17. As late as November 1995, the Prelate of the Methodist Church in the country, the Reverend Sunday Mbang, predicted that the Abacha transition programme would fail without June 12. For him "if they (junta) think they can sweep it under the carpet, they are deceiving themselves", In short, whereas the church hierarchy was visibly concerned about the political health of *La Cite*, the same could not be said about the mosque. The Sultan of Sokoto, Ibrahim Dasuki - who would later be deposed in April 1996 - vacillated endlessly on a firm stand on June 12. There were, however, groups and individuals from the mosque who stood their ground.

to them to either maintain law and order or be disgraced out of power. The case of the traditional rulers was a much easier one. Already used to being pawns in the chessboard of military politics, particularly Babangida's, whose regime also corrupted them through illegal use of public funds, they readily offered to douse the fire of rage and protests in several parts of the country.

Apparently, northern emirs had a bigger assignment to do. Early July 1993, many of them arrived Abuja apparently with the junta's mandate to speak to northern legislators in the NRC and SDP on the need to support Babangida in order to prevent Abiola, a Yoruba man, from getting the presidency. It was even said that "a leading Emir sent a message that an SDP government would marginalise Hausa-Fulani."[108] To achieve this aim, the junta successfully infiltrated the ranks-and-file of the National Assembly (House of Representatives and the Senate). Thus, neither of the two houses had a quorum when a motion supportive of June 12 sponsored by Senate majority leader, Professor Wande Abimbola, was to be discussed. The motion read as follows:

> The Senate now considers the presidential election held on Saturday 12 June 1993 and hereby resolves to uphold the result and urge the federal military government to declare the remaining result of the election; that the president-elect arising from the presidential election of Saturday 12 June 1993 should be sworn in on 27 August 1993.[109]

---

[108] I am here borrowing from Abdulkadir Daiyabu's "The Impasse in Retrospect," *Special* p. 40.

[109] *African Concord*, 19 July 1993, p. 16.

It was, however, in his dealings with the two parties that Babangida was in his best elements. Rather predictably, the NRC offered less resistance lending credence to the wide speculation that Babangida was perhaps that party's number one informal member. Some chieftains of that party would later say Babangida would be most welcome, if he so desired, as their civilian presidential candidate. The romance was such that the party easily agreed to a fresh poll. Once an Interim National Government (ING) was mooted, the party said it would consider it as a viable option only if it got choice positions; otherwise it would support a new election. Yet, Tofa's pre-election promise to adhere to the poll result, whatever it was, ran counter to his party's post-annulment position. He had said that "if we lose (the election) I will thank God, I have done my best. If SDP wins, we will thank God. I think Chief Abiola has actually done his best. I am just taking it easy. I want to retire to my private life. I don't want any problem."[110]

It is quite possible that Tofa spoke the foregoing words in all sincerity. He may not have understood the intricacies of the political game and its stakes having not really been, not unlike Abiola, his chief opponent,, a foundation party man. Rather than immediately concede defeat and congratulate Abiola, he moved from his Kano home to Abuja, going first to *Aso Rock* (the seat of power) before retiring to his hotel suite. A lot transpired in-between; Tofa came out singing a clearly different tune. To all appearances, he started acting out the Babangida-ABN script. According to Davies, while ABN was going on to scuttle the transition, "Bashir Tofa was instructed to insist that the election be cancelled..." On its part, government

---

[110] Cited in *African Concord*, 28 June 1993, p. 28.

would "start lobbying the traditional rulers, governors...to accept the new agenda (of fresh poll)."[111]

For all of the foregoing, many well-known politicians in the SDP and traditional rulers insisted on the June 12 mandate and courageously asked Babangida to install Abiola. The signal from this stance to the military president was that it would be more difficult to break the ranks of the SDP. For one, Abiola was too important a world-wide personality to be treated shabbily in his own country. For another - and more importantly - it was the first time the progressive fraction of the political class was capturing power and it was generally thought that it would give up a good and spirited fight to defend its long-awaited capture of power. But the Nigerian electorate was soon disappointed.

The SDP, we have alluded to this earlier, was a hodgepodge of rabid radicals, progressives, liberals and conservatives who woke up one day to find themselves in the same party because the military licensed only two parties, its own creation. Chief Abiola best epitomised this strange bed-fellow phenomenon. With investments in no fewer than 120 countries by 1990 (45), Abiola was already a scion of the largely feudalo-conservative ruling National Party of Nigeria (NPN) during the Second Republic. He left the party angrily after failing in his nomination bid as presidential candidate and after Umaru Dikko, Shagari's transport minister had told him that the presidency was not for sale. Thus, Abiola, like Yar'Adua, Nzeribe, Falae and so many others in the SDP, had no history or antecedents of radical political struggle. They only had a marriage of

---

[111] A. Davies, "How We Were Used," *African Concord*, 26 July 1993 p. 18-19.

convenience with the radical or progressive tendency in the SDP with a view to capturing political power.

Babangida skilfully exploited this weak point in Abiola. On invitation, the latter was at *Aso Rock* on July 3, 1993. Babangida swore on the Holy Koran that he was not responsible for the annulment. He was quoted as saying to Abiola, his personal friend of some two decades, that if he had declared the results "they would have killed us both."[112] Abiola replied that he did not believe him. He would later refer to the political use to which Babangida put their meeting as "high-wired politics". To selected members of the SDP national executive committee who came a few days later for one of the many mainly nocturnal meetings of that period, Babangida reported the Abiola visit to them "in the strictest confidence". According to an observer "the SDP chieftains read veiled hints and innuendoes in the story and concluded that something was going on behind their back."[113]

The uncertainty thus generated partly explains why the party leaders softened their initial hard stance, obliging to an interim government with NRC. Other factors were also clearly at work. There was the Yar'Adua presidential ambition; thus his position at a key SDP Elders meeting in Benin in July 1993 was to dump Abiola. That position was adopted by the party's executive committee. This was hardly surprising. After Kingibe - another acolyte of Yar'Adua - Anenih, a retired police officer, became the party's chairman. He spearheaded divisions in that party

---

[112] Abiola said as much as guest speaker at the November 1990 Conference of the Nigerian Society for International Affairs (NSIA) held at the Institute of International Affairs, Lagos. The theme of that Conference was "Nigeria's Economic Diplomacy".

[113] See Ike Okonta "The Great Betrayal", *Tempo* 19 July 1993 p? 14-21

and was, alongside other Yar'Adua's protégés, a key player in shaping the contours of an interim government. The latter was nothing, but a diarchy of sorts; a continuation of Babangida regime by other means.

Many Nigerians received the news of SDP's acceptance of the interim government idea with much disappointment. Lewis Obi captures their mood when he argued that

> ...the tragedy is that politicians who should show leadership and adopt principled stand seemed to have reduced the issue to the Roman drama - when the praetorian guards put up the Empire for sale.[114]

Bala Takaya, former university teacher and a front-line member of the SDP, disqualified at the last-minute from contesting gubernatorial elections in Adamawa state in December 1991 and mentioned in high quarters as a probable running mate to Abiola, has argued that SDP problems were not only mainly internal but also rooted in the politics of its formation. For him, there were two groups in the party, the progressives and "those sent to destabilise the party", a subtle reference to the Nzeribe-Yar'Adua axis. He contends that "Abiola won the election but he did not belong to that group that was sent from the reactionary front to hijack our victory and so it was annulled." He also believes that the reactionary group had its roots in the faceless *Kaduna Mafia*. For him, "this cabal does not believe in democracy unless they are in control. Being feudalistic and as such exploitative, democracy is anathema

[114] Lewis Obi "Politicians and History (1)", *African Concord*, 19 July 1993, p. 42

to the Kaduna Mafia." Hence his major argument that the annulment was sponsored by the Kaduna Mafia.[115]

The Babangida regime was at the same time playing the ethnic card. The grand strategy, at this level, was to revisit the civil war and re-open the wounds of an alleged Yoruba betrayal of the Igbo on the eve of the declaration by Ojukwu of the ill-fated Biafran republic, 1967-70. The question posed was "do the Igbo want to fight the cause of the Yoruba for them?" The junta put to dangerously ethnic use not only Uche Chukwumerije, the information secretary and Biafra's deputy propaganda chief but also the former Biafran leader, Emeka Ojukwu, himself. The latter had just become effectively rehabilitated through the complete repossession of his late father's estates in Lagos, the ownership of which was, until then, being contested in court. Ojukwu was given a lot of air time on both the Federal Radio Corporation of Nigeria (FRCN) and the Nigerian Television Authority (NTA) to launch a veritable campaign of calumny against the Yoruba nationality. He alleged, on several occasions, that tracts of war-mongering were being published "somewhere in Ogun state", the home-state of Abiola.

Chukwumerije, who would later become a senator of the Federal Republic of Nigeria at the advent of the Fourth Republic in May 1999, was the veritable linchpin in this ethnic game. He delivered, in a spate of six weeks or so, what amounted to a master-stroke of ethnic conspiracy against the Yoruba. Speaking, for instance, in Kano in July 1993, Chukwumerije asked the north to ally with the East to break the so-called stranglehold of the Lagos-Ibadan

---

[115] See interview "Kaduna Mafia are greedy and selfish - Takaya" *African Concord* 20 December 1993 p. 20-21. See also Takaya and Tyoden (1987) and A.O. Olukoshi (1995).

press on the nation's media industry. There was, indeed, a veritable media game of publicity counter-offensive. The junta attempted to control the print media as well as reinforce its superiority in the electronic media. Thus, in late July 1993, it closed down six media houses (including Abiola's *Concord* titles; *The Punch* and, for a while, the Ogun State Television (OGTV). The aim was to criminalise the Lagos-Ibadan press in the eyes of the reading and listening public. The Babangida junta even contemplated sponsoring two rival national dailies as well as funding a rival human rights group.[116]

In August 1993, the information secretary was seemingly in his best elements. Speaking in Owerri, the Imo state capital, he argued that "Eastern interests do not fit into those of the so-called southern solidarity" against the north. His rationale was that vis-à-vis the Yoruba, the Igbo were clearly a disadvantaged ethnic stock. Thus, his disingenuous argument that the Yoruba

> inhabit the most infrastructurally, industrially and educationally developed axis in black Africa with an enviable network of modem airports, roads, seaports, flyovers, universities, industries and finance houses.

He went as far as insinuating that the Yoruba exploited the misfortunes of the Igbo during the civil war as well as the indigenisation programme of the 1970s.[117] Taken together with the Ojukwu *demarche,* the ultimate aim appeared to be the destruction of the Yoruba civilisation by provoking the nationality to war. In the same vein, by

---

[116] Personal information.

[117] See, for instance, *Third Eye on Sunday* (Ibadan) 5 September 1993 pp. 1, 3.

urging leading Igbo political lights to run in a new presidential poll, the junta wanted the Igbo, in case of victory, to undertake a historic revenge on the Yoruba.[118]

Closely tied to the revenge mission thesis was a clear attempt to isolate western Nigeria and the Yoruba from the country's so-called political mainstream. The propaganda was that an Abiola presidency would engender what Mohammed Haruna refers to as "a Yoruba exclusivist reign". While recognising that such fears "may have merely provided an excuse for delaying the return of the military to the barracks", Haruna nonetheless argues that "those fears are real." He adds that

> ...to the extent that certain sections of the press (again, reference is to the Lagos-Ibadan press) contributed in creating or fuelling those fears, to that extent must they accept responsibility for the

---

[118] Not many, Igbo politicians and related groups sanctioned the politics of ethnicisation of the June 12 election. For instance, the Igbo Forum, the Obi of Onitsha and the Igbo Professional and Business Group dissociated themselves from the mediatory parade of Igbo traditional rulers to Babangida. The Forum argued that since the chiefs visited the General in their private capacities, they could not have spoken for the Igbo people. The Forum also asked the three secretaries of Igbo origin - Akpamgbo (Attorney-General), Nwabueze (Education) and Chukwumerije (Information) - to quit the government. Their argument was that "the market is over and all buyers and sellers are already on their way home". The Professional and Business group notably condemned the search for an Igbo presidential candidate, contending that "majority of Igbo do not support the surreptitious search for the so-called consensus Eastern or Igbo presidential candidate ..." For it, to do this will only succeed in making the Igbo canon fodder in the present political quagmire" See K. Mustapha "On the Brink of Catastrophe" *Tempo* 9 August 1993 pp. 12-13.

probable postponement of our rendezvous with
democracy.[119]

Whatever else anybody or group had against the June
12 election, hardly anyone could, in good conscience, say it
was an ethnic or sub-national affair. Neither could the
ensuing struggle, in the immediate aftermath of its
annulment, be so regarded. According to a view,

> ...the country is fortunate that unlike previous
> crises, the dispute (of annulment) is neither ethnic
> nor religious. It is not between the military and the
> civil population. Most military men are shocked and
> embarrassed by the action of their leaders and
> compatriots.

Ake (1993) also argues that:

> ...when the people revolted on June 12, 1993
> voting against ethnic, regional and religious
> parochialism all those things which the elite uses to
> divide and to manipulate them a monumental crisis
> ensued.[120]

The ethnicisation was a fight-back; a direct reaction to
the crisis Ake refers to on three fronts. The first was
Babangida and his closest entourage of political soldiers
who, save for isolated pockets, wanted their boss to
continue in power for as long as possible. On the second
level was the feudalo-conservative faction of the country's
ruling oligarchy with tentacles nation-wide but

---

[119] M. Haruna "How the Press undermined June 12" *The Citizen* June
28, 1993 p.8. The author heaped the blame of the impasse on the
Ibadan-based Awolowo-owned *Nigerian Tribune*.

[120] See note 47.

headquartered in the core and Far North - the political north. Its eyes were opened to the gravity of the danger of losing political power only when the militarist foot workings to stop Abiola became coterminous with the desperation to halt the Yoruba from adding political power to bureaucratic-economic and intellectual power which, according to the propaganda, had been their preserve since juridical independence in 1960. It would appear that there was mixed success at these two levels. To be sure, Babangida was forced to "step aside" primarily because of a crack within the ranks of his military acolytes and supporters and, secondarily, because of intense pressures from national civil society and key foreign governments. Yet, the fact that Shonekan and, later Abacha, and not Abiola, took over power after Babangida testifies to some success on the part of anti-June 12 elements. Immense state resources and political power of incumbency were put to effective use for the groups concerned, even though to wholly anti-national ends.

The third and last front where the ethnicisation of June 12 was resisted was where it recorded the least success - or, perhaps more correctly, worst failure. That was at the level of Abiola, his entourage and pro-June 12 activists. They all seemingly fell into the trap set by their politico-ideological-opponents, namely, isolating June 12 protagonists, removing the rug from under their feet and portraying them as sectional leaders, who wanted to rule Nigeria at all costs and by all means. As the last days of the Babangida regime copiously showed, the national import of June 12 started wearing off, while the onus was placed on Abiola and his entourage to maintain law and order. The junta's propaganda song was that no individual (reference to Abiola) was greater than the nation. By this time, Abiola was already in Europe ostensibly to solicit support for his mandate. His entourage, because it was a mixture of the good, the bad and the ugly, politically and ideologically speaking, did not, perhaps could not, articulate a coherent national response to the junta's propaganda.

In a fundamental sense, the junta and its sympathisers exploited Abiola's personality as well as his extremely non-combative antecedents to discredit his mandate. Asked in May 1994, at a time there were frenzied preparations for his eventually ill-fated self-declaration as president, why he did not lay claim to his mandate earlier, he replied:

> I don't want bloodshed, I don't want civil war, I want Nigeria intact...I must do nothing that will detract from the integrity of the Nigerian sovereignty as a nation. So, it doesn't matter whether it takes 12 months or more...The important thing is the unity and the sanctity of the country.[121]

But that was exactly the discourse of hegemony of the junta. Abiola seemed to have missed the point that peace and unity are hardly present where and when much store is not set by social justice and equity.

Abiola's pacifist, if not conservative, past was not necessarily an albatross; indeed, had he skilfully exploited this political capital to articulate *a political response of silence* to the annulment, perhaps others would have been propelled to pick up the gauntlet on his behalf.[122] Abiola

---

[121] *African Concord* 6 June 1994 p. 18. Cf. Obi's argument that "those who have worked hardest to destroy Nigeria are now the most vociferous in affirming their belief in its 'corporate existence'. In his "The Nigerian Tragedy (3): Dishonest rulers" *African Concord* 22 November 1993 p. 34.

[122] Former Head of State, General Olusegun Obasanjo, said this much while discussing with this writer and two editors of a national

failed to follow through this path to the end. His disappointment was understandable, having, as he claimed, been assured by Babangida that the latter was ready to vacate the presidency and hand over power. Yet, by an admixture of tactlessness and political naivety, Abiola gradually undermined his own historic mandate. Any pertinent analysis cannot but wonder aloud what his immediate politico-ideological and strategic entourage did to limit the damage.

For one, Abiola was too loud, both inside and outside the country -but particularly in the latter, via *CNN et al.* - in defending his mandate. Rather tactlessly, it was the political North that became the butt of his tirades. For another, he seemed not to have understood that his worst enemies were in his party, the SDP, and these were not necessarily the most visibly hostile. His uncomplimentary

---

newspaper in his Otta farms in early 1994. He claimed to have phoned Abiola from London soon after the annulment, urging him to hold his peace and *Siddon Look* (that is, hold your peace and say and do nothing). He said he was disappointed a few days later to read an Abiola outburst that 'the North did not want me to rule' or something like that. Obasanjo and Abiola were schoolmates at the Baptist Boys High School, Abeokuta, their home-town, but could hardly have been described as the best of friends. Obasanjo, who allegedly sold the idea of an interim government to Babangida, may not have wanted an Abiola presidency. So also was General Yakubu Gowon who (according to one of his confidants, one of his ministers whom I spoke with in Abuja in September 1994) still has scores to settle with Abiola. He believes, apparently without any convincing shreds of evidence, that Abiola was a co-financier of the palace coup of July 29, 1975 that ousted him from power. The coup was masterminded by then Brigadier Joseph Garba, Gowon's head of presidential brigade of guards and General Mohammed, his immediate replacement. This explains why there is no record anywhere showing that Gowon spoke against the annulment or, for that matter, urged the authorities to install Abiola as president.

remarks about some of his associates made public on the eve of the first year of the annulment when these people were already in power in the Abacha junta may have been whispered much earlier, with all the imagined consequences.

About Kingibe, his running-mate and Abacha's first foreign affairs minister (and, later, internal affairs), Abiola said:

> At the time I picked him as a running mate, he was an ordinary member of the SDP. Politically...he was of no relevance...I offered him the running mate position which he accepted in public and apparently happily.

Told that big names like Jakande had accepted to serve under Abacha, Abiola replied: "What big name? The only big name in politics of Nigeria today is MKO, voted for overwhelmingly by the Nigerian people." And referring generally to politicians in both the SDP and the NRC serving in the Abacha regime, he said:

> they have been lying to themselves thinking that they are democrats, when in fact they are just opportunists, political prostitutes, harlots, that's what they are.[123]

Furthermore, Abiola did not seem to understand the ways and manners of politicians, both civil and military put together. For instance, he did not have to seek permission from Abacha, soon after the latter's palace coup, to hold a political meeting in his house. Even if he did, as he later confessed, did he have to make it public? He reported back

---

[123] All the quotations cited in *African Concord* 6 June 1994 p.20.

to Abacha, informing him that his people - meaning his political associates - said he should hold on to his mandate. Thereafter, this dialogue ensued:

Abacha: "How do you want to hold on to your mandate, when I want to rule?"

Abiola: "Well, I will obey the people, not you. In any case, you told me you voted for me on that day. So, I'm obeying you among the others who voted for me."[124]

This political naivety was, on the ground, translated into excessive trust and confidence in the same civilo-military gladiators who had either annulled his election or who were determined to assist the junta consign it to the dustbin of history. Abiola and his entourage drafted an address Abacha promised to read in his inaugural broadcast to de-annul the election. This was to have been informed, *inter alia*, by the deteriorating corporate image of the armed forces since the annulment, to wit, "the Nigerian armed forces and government have become a subject of ridicule, harassment, distrust and even dishonour, at home and abroad."[125] Abacha never read the address. Rather, he, like Shonekan before him, affirmed that June 12 was dead. Whilst abroad, Abiola was reaching out to Shonekan and allegedly agreed not to come home on September 12, 1993 as previously announced. According to the secretary to the interim government, Alhaji Mustapha Umara, Abiola agreed with Shonekan that "his return at that time may be exploited by mischief-makers to create confusion."[126] Yet, many young people had died on the streets of Lagos protesting the annulment and demanding for its reinstatement.

---

[124] Ibid., p. 21-22.

[125] Ibid., *passim*.

[126] *Third Eye on Sunday* 12 September 1993 p. 1, 10.

There was yet another evidence of lack of political sagacity: Abiola's letter to Babangida, entitled *Let's be friends again*, soliciting for the general's intervention to claim his mandate. Abiola notably wrote: "I am saddened by the way all you have achieved in office have been rubbished by many of those who have enjoyed your confidence and generosity."[127] Apparently the result of earlier exchanges, Babangida was expected to address a press conference in Minna, his home-town, and make public, details of the annulment, the act of which was to be located beyond Babangida, extending blame to Abacha. True to type, Babangida backed out of the arrangement at the last minute. Rather, the document was leaked to military authorities who passed it on to Abiola's staunch supporters and to the press.

The consequences of the foregoing development were predictable. One, Abiola and his entourage were unable or unwilling - or both - to seize on the moment to recover the presidential mandate, in particular during the vacuum created by the judiciary's declaration of the interim government as illegal.

Two, the fragility of the Abiola camp was such that whilst the Babangida and Shonekan governments were fragmenting, an alternative coalition to govern was not forthcoming.

Civil society's response

Whatever the *faux-pas* of Abiola and his entourage, nothing can detract from the fact than the June 12 election constituted an inviolate political watershed in the country's

---

[127] *Tempo*, 10 March 1994, p. 45.

history. The Nigerian civil society understood this historical reality quite well. I have examined this phenomenon elsewhere (Amuwo, 1995) and it, therefore, need not detain us here. But suffice it to make some apposite observations.

Once it was clear that neither the courts nor the military junta could give relief to the people, the locus of transactional exchanges between the state and civil society shifted to the streets. Fawehinmi captured the character of the response as follows: "We must now make the country totally ungovernable and flush out the enemy of Nigeria from the governance of the country." The Campaign for Democracy (CD), organised a week of national protest from July 4, 1993. The protest was, however, localised to Lagos and some major towns in Oyo, Ogun, Ondo, Osun and Kwara States. Minor protests were recorded in the east, while all was virtually quiet in the north.

It has often been suggested that unlike Latin America, Africa has yet to have mature political institutions and a clearly profiled civil society with articulate social classes and groups. There is also the argument that, as in India, two tendencies at work in the shaping of Nigeria's democracy over time have assailed civil society organisations. These two tendencies are, on the one hand, *more democratisation* through a rise in consciousness and organisation of popular classes and, on the other, *creeping authoritarianism* (Sorensen, 1993:20, 26). By the same token, Bratton (cited in Gerber, 1994:7-9) has argued that NGOs in Africa have tended to replicate in society an illiberal political culture of the state.

Space - but certainly not time - will not permit us to consider the merits and demerits of these arguments. It should be conceded, however, that military authoritarianism, particularly rampant and severe in the dying days of the Babangida regime, was brought to bear on the protests. Armoured tanks were rolled out on the orders of Abacha, then Shonekan's defence secretary. Many souls, particularly young people, were lost.

There is certainly something deplorable in the conduct of protests by the Nigerian civil society. Randall Robinson put the matter succinctly recently: "When the leader is detained, the group collapses."[128] The junta was very much aware of this organisational weakness. It incarcerated, amongst others, Fawehinmi, Femi Falana, Beko Ransome-Kuti and Ozekhome, scions of the emergent civil society. During the oil workers strike in July and August 1994, the arrest and detention of Chief Frank Kokori, secretary general of the national union of petroleum and natural gas workers (NUPENG) was one of the reasons for the early collapse of the strike. Often missing are organisational linkages among the diverse social components of the country's opposition movement. But this is certainly not the same thing as saying that protesters in the west should, on the June 12 annulment, have liaised with their colleagues elsewhere in the federation in order to ensure a total onslaught. Citizens properly so-called ought not to be prompted to defend their inalienable rights.

By way of conclusion

The foregoing notes on the antagonistic struggles to recover the June 12 presidential mandate of Abiola and to consign to history's dustbin suggest that whilst one group (anti-June

---

[128] Cited in "Commonwealth Slams Sanctions," *Nigerian Tribune*, April 25, 1996, p. 1, 2.

12) sought maintenance of the current lopsided socio-economic formation and social relations, the other (pro-June 12) was fighting to ensure a decomposition of the latter as well as re-composition of a new one.[129] As Weyland (1995) reasons in respect of Latin America, liberalism often flounders to populism partly because "widespread poverty makes large numbers of people susceptible to benefits guaranteed by clientelism and to populist slogans." The poor here consists not only of a huge army of the perpetually impoverished, but, perhaps more significantly, of an assorted array of professional politicians, contractors and businessmen who, because they constantly need a lot of state-driven resources to maintain their expensive lifestyle, often throw their otherwise lofty political values and principles to the dogs on the altar of political and economic expediency.

I have limited my analysis to the immediate period of the annulment. But there is a rich data waiting to be tapped from the annulment through Shonekan to Abacha governments. The point is that the politicisation of June 12 election was growing monstrously by the day. Even in the early days in 1993, the notable Nigerian playwright, Ola Rotimi, did make the important observation that

> ...the longer this matter of 12 June is allowed to drag on, the wider the space for self-serving groups to bustle in, fanning atavistic embers of tribalism and sectionalism designed to contain truth and perpetuate chaos.[130]

---

[129] M. Braton and N. de Walle (1992) envisage a deconstruction-reconstruction scenario analogous to that of decolonisation - nation building.

[130] Ola Rotimi, 'Military, Religion and 12 June," in *Special* p. 13.

Yet, Nigeria cannot afford *not* to become a democracy in the emergent twenty-first century. More significantly, Africa's most populous and, arguably, most important country can only develop democratically. There is a lot of work to be done by the country's civil society. But it needs a lot of help from civil societies in other climes and climates, especially in the global south. This is because the struggle to recover June 12 and, ultimately, make the country a democracy is rendered the more difficult by virtue of a nearly suffocating grip of the state on the civil society. Moreover, the latter and social movements "harbour contradictory purposes" to the extent that the "civil society is not just external to the state, rather various and even contradictory groups in the civil society penetrate the state differentially" (Mamdani, 1995: 604-5).

In other words, to translate the pious hopes of a (liberal) democratic Nigeria by many a Nigerian pro-12 June activists and groups to concrete reality, these elements have to be strengthened and empowered in many ways. To ensure the fulfilment of the prophetic statement by a federal government newspaper that "though Nigeria is going through a difficult time...the country will rise from the ashes and be the example of true democracy the world over"[131] Nigerians need more than what the same medium earlier referred to as "renewed faith in a prosperous Nigeria of tomorrow." Nor, is it enough for them to count on their own political, moral and financial resources; these appear increasingly largely inadequate as successive military juntas and their civilian collaborators become more and more desperate.

---

[131] "Between optimism and cynicism," editorial, *Daily Times* (Lagos), March 7, 1996, p.6

References

Ake, C. (I991) "Re-thinking Democracy in Africa" Journal of Democracy, 2, 1, Winter: 32-44.
—— (1992) "Devaluing Democracy" Journal of Democracy, 3, 3, July: 32-36.
———— (1993) "Is Africa Democratizing?" The Guardian Lecture Series, December 12, Nigerian Institute of International Affairs, Lagos.
Amuwo, 'K. (1995) General Babangida Civil Society and the Military in Nigeria: Failure of a Personal Rulership Project, Travaux et Documents, Institut d'Etudes Politiques, (IEP), Centre d'Etudes d'Afrique Noire (CEAN), Universite de Bordeaux, 40 pp
Bratton, M (1992) "Zambia starts over" Journal of Democracy 3, 2   April: 81-94
Bratton M. and N. Van de Walle (1992) "Toward Govemance in Africa: Popular demands and state responses" in G. Hyden and M. Bratton (eds) Governance and Politics in Africa (Boulder and London: L. Rienner Publishers):27-56.
Dahl R. (1992) "The Problem of Civic Competence" Journal of Democracy 3, 4 October: 45-59.
Frischtak, L. (1994) Governance Capacity and Economic Reform in Developing Countries World Bank Technical paper, Number 254
Gerber D. (1994) "African NGOS: A Plus for Democracy and Development?" Africa Democracy and Development 3, 3, September: 7-9.
Geremek B (1992) "Civil Society, Then and Now" Journal of Democracy 3, 2, April: 3-12.
Mamdani, M. (1995) "A Critique of the State and Civil Society Paradigm in Africanist Studies" in Mamdani and Wamba-dia-Wamba (eds) African Studies in Social Movements and Democracy (Dakar; Codesria Books): 602-616.
Olukoshi, A.0. (1995) "Bourgeois Social Movements and the Struggle for Democracy in Nigeria: An Inquiry into the 'Kaduna Mafia''' in Mamdani and Wamba-dia-Wamba, African Studies in Social Movements: 245-278.
Ottaway, M. (1995) "Democracy and the Challenge of Ethnicity" Africa Demos, III, 4, March: 22-24.
Plattner M. F. (1992) "Exploring the End of History" rev. article of F. Fukuyama's The End of History and The Last Man 1992 in Journal of Democracy 3, 2, April: 118-121.
Sanguinetti J.M. (1991) "Present at the transition" Journal of Democracy, 2, l. Winter: 3-10
Sartori G. (1 995) "How far can free Government travel?" Journal of Democracy, 6, 3, July: 101-111.

Sorensen G. (1993) "Democracy, Authoritarianism and State Strength" European Journal of Development Research 5, 1 June: 6-34.

Takaya B. and S.G. Tyoden eds. (1987) The Kaduna Maria: A Study of the Rise, Development and Consolidation of a Nigerian Power Elite, Jos: Jos University Press

Weyland, K (1995) "Latin America's Four Political Models", Journal of Democracy, 6, 4: 125-139